RAISE THE SAILS

Copyright ©Sid Oakley, 2009. All rights rese rved. No part of this book may be reproduced or transmitted in any form or by any means, electronic or mechanical, including photocopying, recording, or by any information storage and retrieval system, without permission in writing from the publisher.

Millennial Mind Publishing
An imprint of American Book Publishing
5442 So. 900 East, #146
Salt Lake City, UT 84117-7204
www.american-book.com
Printed in the United States of America on acid-free paper.

Raise the Sails

Designed by Dimitar Bochukov, design@american-book.com

Publisher's Note: *American Book Publishing relies on the author's integrity of research and attribution; each statement has not been investigated to determine if it has been accurately made. The author and publisher specifically disclaim any responsibility for any liability, loss, or risk, personal or otherwise, which is incurred as a consequence, directly or indirectly, of the use and application of any of the contents of this book. In such situations where medical, legal, or other professional services may apply, please seek the advice of such professionals directly.*

Library of Congress Cataloging-in-Publication Data
Oakley, Sid.
Raise the sails / Sid Oakley.
   p. cm.
ISBN-13: 978-1-58982-489-8
ISBN-10: 1-58982-489-X
1. Oakley, Sid. 2. Sailors--United States--Biography. I. Title.
GV812.5.O35A2 2009
797.1092--dc22
[B]
                    2008040578
Special Sales

These books are available at special discounts for bulk purchases. Special editions, including personalized covers, excerpts of existing books, and corporate imprints, can be created in large quantities for special needs. For more information e-mail info@american-book.com.

*Tom & Louisa —
Raise the Sails in
your life
  Sid*

RAISE THE SAILS

Sid Oakley

Raise the Sails
The wind blows where it will, that's not of our choosing.
You can just sit still, and not know what you'd be losing,

So raise the sails, or you will never leave the shore,
You may feel safe but you will never know, if there was more
So raise the sails.

The wind blows where it will; the power can be frightening.
You can feel it build, storm, thunder, and lightning,

So raise the sails, trust that strength to drive you on
To things you could never do, all on your own
So raise the sails.

The wind blows where it will, beyond all comprehension.
Follow it until you reach your destination,

So raise the sails, reach out to the wind,
Listen as it guides you on, the journey begins.

So raise the sails, let the Spirit set you free
To sail beyond horizon's bonds, it's your opportunity
So raise the sails.

The wind blows where it will
So raise the sails.
Words and Music by Mike Bramble

Preface

After the half-century marker rose tall from a speck on the horizon, and the time had passed when a mood recaptured was an inspiration, I found myself together with those who had lost their way. As had many before me, I had abandoned a god who seemed most conspicuous by his absence in favor of my own wisdom and such popular counsel as was available. Believing in little, ridiculing much, and standing for nothing, I began to contemplate if mine was a life worth living.

Had anyone asked me a few years ago, I would have said that *Silk Purse* saved my life, and I suppose she did have a part in it. I might not have postponed my own demise long enough for an intervention had I not become distracted by sailing and obsessed with *Silk Purse*. Today I would give a different answer to that question. To those who would have today's answer now, I ask for a measure of patience and offer a story of sails, discovery, and grace. I do have one request. Please, as you read this, try to remember that a lot of what happened was Doug's fault.

Table of Contents

1. Legacy	1
2. Theme Song	7
3. Well-Informed Start	13
4. Selection Process	23
5. Labor Pains	31
6. A Beginning	35
7. Whistling in the Dark	43
8. You Can't Learn It from a Book	53
9. Cutting the Cord	67
10. Going Solo	81
11. Abaco Cruising	93
12. Oh Savannah!	109
13. At Last	129
14. Coastal Cruising	135
15. Hope	141
16. Your Watch	145
17. Knockdown, Drag Out	153
18. Enroute	165
19 Mecca	171

20. Staniel Cay Back	183
21. Inflection Point	191
22. Last Leg	205
23. Update	213
Glossary	217
Acknowledgements	225

Chapter 1: *Legacy*

When the gray fog of depression gathers, you become aware of the legacy. It condenses, darkening and obscuring all light. It continues to descend, gaining weight and substance until you are wrapped to near paralysis in a dread, black shroud. You begin to fear the legacy. Finally, Satan sits cross-legged on your chest, bends down, and whispers in your ear. You can feel the sound scratching through your ear into your throat and down.

"Come on, come on. You know what to do. Come on."

The truth of the legacy is that you do know what to do.

JANUARY 1974

It is amazing how a shotgun blast fired from two rooms away sounds so unlike what we expect. We didn't hear the loud boom of the discharge. We didn't feel its energy in the air around us when my father laid his Winchester twelve gauge across his desk and blew a hole in his chest that you could reach your hand through. Instead, we heard what sounded like the sharp crack of a paddle smacked against his wooden desktop. Nevertheless, my mother, brother, and I were frozen in the chill that always surrounds the unspoken understanding of a truth too terrible to speak.

A spaghetti western played on the television. Clint Eastwood's man with no name tossed his cigar butt into the dust, squinted into the bright light, and then gunned down two tough-looking hombres before their guns cleared their holsters. The shots from his colt .45 made a whining ricochet sound. No ricochet sound came from the senior Sidney Oakley's twelve gauge as the double-ought shot slammed into its mark.

If you had been in my parent's home over the days preceding his exit, you would have realized that my father was unstable and possibly suicidal. The atmosphere in the little house was as thick with tension as the summer-like air was heavy with humidity. A wet steaming towel of resignation hung over our heads and shoulders, bowing our backs and giving the air we breathed the thick, cloying taste of impending disaster.

In fact, only a couple of days before Doug and I had discussed getting the twelve-gauge shells out of the house. Not that we really thought we could stop him, but possibly we could have tested his conviction by making things a little more difficult. I, at least, half-expected my father's final action, but in no way were any of us prepared for the shock of it. So it was that the sound of the Winchester's crack caught the three of us by complete surprise, followed by a spontaneous understanding. . .

I entered my father's office with the sulphurous odor of burnt cordite stinging my nose and a light fog of smoke hanging in the air. A thick oily fear painted the back of my throat with the taste of cod liver and bile. With all my heart, I wanted to run out my mom's front door, get in my car, and drive back to Atlanta where I could pretend that what I was about to see never happened. My mind revved into high gear racing for a way to delay, if only for a moment, confronting what must be confronted.

At first, I didn't see him, and I dropped low in the doorway glancing left toward the adjoining bedroom. To this day I don't know if I more expected to see dear old dad there, shotgun poised waiting for one of us, or the intruder who must have broken into the house and done this thing I was about to witness.

I mention an intruder because no matter how much I'm anticipating something horrible, something unspeakable, when it does arrive, I have a limitless ability to lie to myself. Suicide? My father would never work that dark trick on us. Would he? He knew about suicide; he knew first hand about the carnage it left in a family. Years before, his father had exited life through that same door. A twelve gauge was as effective in 1934 as it was in 1974.

But there was no intruder. Our father had engineered the act himself, and it wasn't difficult to reconstruct the sequence of events. Across the top of the desk that dominated his office, lay his Winchester pump. A breath of smoke still wafted from its chamber. I went behind the desk. From the smeared blood and tissue on the wall, it was clear that the blast had flung him from his chair and slammed him against the rear wall. He had come to rest in somewhat of a prayer position on the hardwood floor with his head stuffed in the metal trash can he kept in the corner. My first thoughts were about how thankful I was that Mother would not have to erase that sight from her mind. It would be some time later before I was to learn that she had seen it all.

I fought back the panic that still screamed inside my head. If I could just get to the car, just get out of there, it would all go away. For the first time, I became aware of my brother's presence behind me. He both gave me courage and blocked my retreat. I rolled the chair out of the way and bent over our father. I stretched him out on his back as the trashcan rolled to one side. There was life in his eyes.

"Daddy, please live," I heard myself say.

At that very instant, I recognized the biggest lie I had ever told: I didn't want him to live. I wanted to somehow manage to push him into that trashcan and be done with it. He and his alcoholism had robbed me of my childhood and much of my adolescence. Now he was threatening to steal away another part of my life just as I was beginning to climb from my hole. Pictures of providing convalescent care for this man that I had grown to both despise from experience, and love from a sense of obligation filled my mind. I wanted a lot of things for the three of us, and for me, that Sunday night, but the survival of Gilbert Sidney Oakley, Sr. wasn't one of them. I got my wish. I need not have worried. The light went out in my father's eyes. I hoped he didn't recognize the lie, and I pray that I never again have the need to repeat anything like that verse of the *Pater Noster*.

"Doug," I said. "Give him mouth to mouth or something. I'll call an ambulance."

I knew that CPR was a waste of time, and I was sure my brother did as well. But something had to be done and I could not bear the thought of touching my father again. I beat a retreat from the office with our hysterical mother in tow. I dialed zero and asked for the police. I remember the surprise I felt at my calm demeanor. My voice did not crack or sound hoarse or weak.

"Police Department." The bored voice came across the line.

"I need an ambulance and an officer over here quickly," I said, still under control. "My father just shot himself."

"Oh my God! When?" The male voice sputtered and took on a pitch suitable for the last walk down death row. "I mean where? What's your name? My God!"

It was then that I noticed the shaking receiver in my hand, the tremor in my own voice, and the perspiration bursting from every pore. My shirt was instantly soaked, sweat ran from my brow in rivulets, but no moisture escaped from my eyes. I had no tears for Senior. I told myself then that they would come: the tears and tremors of shock. They had to, didn't they? I wasn't so certain. I looked into my own heart that night and had dimly recognized, but not cared for what I had seen. I simply knew that the picture was one of sorrow rather than grief.

We dealt with ambulance, police, doctors, and the hospital, while each of us viewed the events of the evening through a haze of shock and guilt. When the last policeman had gone and the last form was completed, we pulled the mattresses off all three beds in the house and made them up on the living room floor. We spent what remained of the senior Gilbert Sidney Oakley's last day on earth huddled together. Our only defense against the demons was each other's presence.

I did not realize then that with his last act my father had bequeathed to me the legacy shared by all children of a successful suicide. That is, the certain knowledge that no matter how circumstances and the world might align themselves against us, there is always a way out. We are always in control of our final destiny. My father's name was Sidney. His father's name was Sidney. My name is Sidney. I know the truth of the legacy. It is an inheritance that I have been required to reject more than once. I beg God that my brother has rejected it as well.

"Come on, come on. You know what to do."

Chapter 2: *Theme Song*

JULY 1994

It's late July 1994, and I'm sitting at my desk in Kennesaw, Georgia daydreaming about being in Florida when the phone summons me back to reality.

"Sid Oakley," I said into the thing, trying as best I could to inject some enthusiasm I didn't feel.

"Hey Bro, it's Doug." A somber voice slipped from the receiver.

I responded with dumbfounded silence, partially because at that moment Henry Mancini's *Theme from Peter Gun* began to play in my head. The tune's driving rhythm had recently become my sailboat tune, *Da-da-da-da, Da-da-da-da*. For those too young to remember the TV show, you're likely to be too young to understand the true meaning of mid-life crisis, which I'll tell you now is one of the themes of this story.

"You know, your brother?" Doug paused as if to let the magnitude of this settle in. "I got bad news."

Bad news? How could he have bad news? Doug was calling from Embree Marine in St. Petersburg where he was watching the delivery of my brand new sailboat, an Island Packet 40, christened *Silk Purse*. And, as you might have guessed, that's exactly why the subject of this morning's daydream has its setting in Florida.

Before going any further, I need to tell you that I had just paid an outrageous sum for this boat. How outrageous? Twenty-five percent more than the value of my house at the time. At least I had arranged with a certifiably insane lending institution to pay for it on the never, never. However, I had been assured by the gentleman who sold it to me that this boat would take me anywhere in the world there was five feet of water. Just imagine, for a little more than the cost of a modest to average suburban house, I could vagabond around the world, see the South China Sea, cruise the canals of France, and retrace the voyages of Sinbad.

This fellow, Sam, who turned out to be a fine person with whom I became friends, conjured up an instant feeling of trust as soon as we met. I could be Sinbad reincarnate, slay a dragon, pillage and plunder. But I digress, which is something I do often, and one of the things I do well. My editor tells me that I should strive not to allow digression to become a theme of this book.

Back to Doug, and back to bad news, any of which must mean *Silk Purse*.

"OK, Doogie, let's have it."

"They dropped your boat."

I didn't answer. There was an ice pick in my throat.

"It slipped off the travel lift when they were pulling it off the delivery truck. When it bounced off the hard (the hard: sailor-talk for dry earth or pavement, usually in a boatyard), the keel cracked."

The ice pick found my heart. Mancini's rhythm slowed to a stop. *Da-da – da- - da . . .*

"They think they can fix it though."

God bless my little brother; he tried so hard to reassure me. You'll just have to suffer through a lot about Doug if all this survives the editor's red pencil. He was my sailing mentor through much of what is to follow and can be held directly responsible for a good bit of it.

"It's on its way back to Packet." Pause. Phone static. I'm searching my desktop—there must be blood somewhere. "Did you pay that insurance premium?"

"Insurance?"

I dropped the receiver on my desk, which is an understandable thing for a multiple stab wound victim. With my heart pounding a double-time version of an unidentified funeral dirge, I bent down toward the desk and shouted into the receiver.

"Fix it? They can't fix that!"

There was no way to fix my boat. They'd have to make me another one. Even I knew that. Oh, did I mention that I couldn't sail this boat? Couldn't drive it. Couldn't park it and had only a limited idea of what a fine piece of cruising boat design and craftsmanship I'd purchased? I didn't think so, but there we go again off on another tangent.

The point is, another boat would mean starting over. It would take time, and I couldn't wait. I was anxious to get to those places with five feet of water. What if, in the time required to get another boat, I came to my senses and dropped the idea of becoming a sailorman, a regular Tristan Jones? Besides, I'd gotten amazingly attached to hull number 22. I had taken a family-sized photo album of pictures during several intervals of her construction, not to mention a full color shot of her emerging from the womb. I'd bought many after-hours beers for the assisting physicians who molded her fiberglass, sanded her joinery, and installed her hardware. Each of these dedicated professionals assured me that my boat would be the finest Island Packet 40 ever fashioned on Wild Acres Road (only confirmed Island Packet groupies know this is the factory address). Hull 22 was *Silk Purse*, and I didn't want another one.

"It's not that big a crack." A familiar voice came from the receiver, which had somehow returned to my hand. "I think they might be able to fix it OK…"

"OK, my –"

"I'm joking, Bro. It's fine."

"If you think—" My lungs bellowed. Blood pounded against my eardrums. "If you think I'm about to settle for a repair job—"

"Sid, Sid. I'm joking, don't hyperventilate." The first undisguised laugh slipped from his little weasel mouth. "Take it easy—it's a joke."

He's in hysterics by now. I can see him slapping his knee and holding up the receiver while he points to it with little weasel type hand motions. He'd make sure every jackleg in that boatyard office knows what a chump his big brother was. What he doesn't realize is that everybody thinks I'm the smart one.

"Man, you are killing me," Doug said, his voice heavy with that tripping sort of laughing quality that adds to the humor of a situation—unless you are the butt of the joke, that is. "The boat is fine. You should see the guys here at the yard—they think you're a funny man."

Yeah, that's me, a regular Bob Hope. It was right then that the plot for my next book began to take shape. *Vengeance: A Brother Strikes Back*. I'm sure it'll be a best seller.

Oh, did I mention that my brother's phone number is 910-555-1812, and he is in dire need of some term life insurance?

Da-da-da-da, Da-da-da-da.

Chapter 3: *Well-Informed Start*

One Year Earlier

Six hundred fifty miles off the North Carolina coast a cluster of islands, known as Bermuda, called to sailors before the United States was even a concept. Doug had been listening to their call for a number of years. When he decided to answer, I found myself responding with a reluctant enthusiasm.

JUNE 1993

The sun climbed high in the cotton ball sky above Mathews Point Marina. Already the mercury was racing up the NuGrape Soda thermometer swinging from a rusty nail driven into the longleaf pine bark. We loaded *Windswept* with as much ice as we could jam into her overtaxed icebox, tossed off her dock lines, and backed out of the slip.

We were off for Bermuda! The trip over was scheduled to take seven days, and promised to be the adventure of my lifetime. Aboard were future sailorman Sid; my brother and captain, Doug; Charles Hardin; and Warren "Cannonball" Kennedy.

Actually, an hour later I was thinking seven days stuck on this thirty-foot Catalina with two friends and my brother was promising to last a lifetime. I was dressed in a starched pair of kaki shorts and a nice Polo shirt. They were dressed in T-shirts and ragged shorts, and talking about how many days they could go without a bath. Glad I brought the Right Guard.

As you might have guessed, I really hadn't developed my sailboat persona yet. I had associated sailing to Bermuda with Stede Bonnet and Blackbeard, yacht club commodores, navy blazers with a crest on the pocket, and the romance of the sea. You know the kinds of things we saw in the movies when we were kids.

There was no wind and we had to motor up the ICW (that's Intracoastal Waterway to you lubbers) at full sailboat speed. *Putt putt putt putt.* Two Jet Ski teenagers zoomed by, then decided it would be fun to buzz donuts around us as we headed toward Beaufort, NC. Next, some sort of turtle passed us, and the teens throttled up their engines, like two chain saws, in hot pursuit of more challenging prey.

"I hate those noisy things," Doug said as he inspected our flare gun and sighted down the barrel like it was a thirty-eight. "Somebody oughta do something about them."

"Are we gonna need that?" I pointed to the strange pistol that actually fired some sort of gauge shotgun shell incendiary device. I envisioned an ignited flare rocketing into the sky and sort of parachuting down to sea. No doubt, this would take place as twenty-foot sharks circled our sinking boat.

Doug just shrugged his shoulders and twisted his lips into a frown. He put the gun back in the canister and sat it down beside him in the cockpit. I went forward—that's toward the pointy end. The sun had climbed toward noon and I looked behind us. I promise the marina was still in easy view.

Putt putt putt putt.

Assured that the bow was secure, I headed back toward the cockpit in time to see the Jet Ski brothers heading back for another buzz around the sailboat. Hey, it's not like they couldn't find us. Weren't we still in the same place?

When I arrived aft, Doug was shifting his eyes from the approaching noise machines to the in-canister flare gun. He stood behind the wheel, and I managed to get between our captain and the ship's arsenal. I had visions of what one of these things could do. I mean, I've seen my share of James Bond movies, and I keep up with advances in military hardware.

I said, "When do you think we'll get there?"

"Get where?" Doug asked and looked ahead, like I was talking about the next marker or something.

"Where? Aren't we going to Bermuda?"

"We haven't even started to Bermuda yet. We'll stop in Beaufort to top off with diesel."

"How far to Beaufort?"

"Shut up and get the captain a beer."

"Aye, sir."

Below, Charles Hardin, my watch captain, was pulling some Vienna (vie-ana) sausages from the icebox. He straightened up and handed me a couple of Miller Lights. I noticed that Charlie looked fairly clean, but then he wasn't my bunkmate so maybe I'd relaxed my standards.

I tossed one of the beers to Doug. "Here, Cap."

Charlie said, "We won't really be on our way to Bermuda until we pass Red Four."

I gave a considered and benign 'the sage was pondering' type nod. All the while I am wondering what in the world was a Red Four? I mean I can picture a four that happens to be red, but I was pretty sure it wasn't that simple.

I said, "Guess that's right. It's Red Four, top off in Beaufort, then tallyho to Bermuda."

Charlie looked at me like I had the plague, so I went to the helm with Doug. As I climbed through the companionway, I realized that even though we had been gone just a few hours I had toured the boat, explored every nook not stuffed with ice, and at least temporarily irritated everyone on board. Myself included. This would be a long trip.

"Doug," the Cannonball said, "I guess we plot a course to Bermuda from Red Four."

"Yeah, no sense in worrying about the sea buoy. We're clear of everything after four."

We did stop in Beaufort and top off our diesel tanks. From there it was a short trip to the channel leading to open ocean. As we approached the Atlantic I noticed a double row of buoys that somehow, through a miracle of technology, managed to float each in its own place. Even I could see that they marked a channel through which boats might have passage across the shoals that lined the Carolina coast. Further someone had thought to paint them—red to the left and green to our right as we surged toward the Atlantic. As we passed through the channel, I noticed that the buoys were also numbered. With the sun dropping below the western horizon there was still enough light for me to read the big black **4** painted on the red buoy we passed to our left.

During all the hours that I've sailed with Doug or anyone else, after all the sea stories, fish stories, near lies, and plain lies; this is the first time that I've admitted that on my first true ocean passage I had no idea what the channel markers were.

Red Four and soon there after the Beaufort Inlet sea buoy slipped from view and we were off to Bermuda, better than six hundred miles across open ocean on *Windswept*—a boat that wasn't exactly made for that type passage. Not that there is a thing wrong with a Catalina, but before we landed in Bermuda we were windswept, sea swept, and out of ice and beer. Several things that looked important shook loose and danced across the decks much in the manner of those old electric football games. Some of them we retrieved, others no.

The first three days on board I thought that I would jump out of my skin. I was caught on a little cork bobbing in the middle of the Atlantic and forced to battle acute tiny boat fever. Doug had described sailing as the ultimate experience of freedom. Those first three days I thought I had been sentenced to a Confederate prison. I was never really sick, but never really well. In any case, time passed slowly in Andersonville. On the fourth day, it got worse; as I became certain that there was a straight jacket in my future. I mean, where was Blackbeard? How about Stede Bonnet? I was in desperate need of something, anything, to plunder.

I tried to act excited, and there were high moments, as can be seen from the following chart notations that our captain made daily as he recorded our position on the nautical chart. That's like a big map of the water.

Day 2 – 33° 57` N/ 74° 32` W Sid takes a bath!!
Day 3 – 33° 18` N/ 72° 32` W Caught first tuna (see pix)

Day 4 – 32° 46` N/ W (illegible) Caught first seabird, released note in bottle, all took showers, boat smells better, Cannonball claims to have seen a Domino's Pizza billboard.

Day 5 – 33°25` N/ 69° 37` W weather building, sleep impossible.

Day 6 – 32° 52`N/ 67°15` W First report of tropical depression #1 from navy pilot, wave tops getting green.

Day 7 – 32° 38` N/ 66°17` W We made it to a new day, sighted Bermuda at 1230 and threw champagne bottle overboard, thanks Sid.

Somewhere on day five, as the weather got worse. Cannonball continued to exhibit symptoms of PDS (pizza deprivation syndrome) demanding that we cook the pepperoni special that he knew we had hidden on the boat.

As the winds began to build and seas grew from hills to mountains, Cannonball careened down the companionway.
"I just saw a Dominos Pizza delivery boat! Some body dial 4-4304."

Although he was never successful in getting the pizza man's attention, my spirits began to pick up. This was due in part to the fact that I had quit taking medication for motion sickness and was no longer drugged into lethargy. Also, I was beginning to contribute to the success of our mission. OK, in tiny little ways like staying awake for at least a part of my watch, or finally understanding that it was **always** clockwise around a winch. (winch: sailor talk for that metal drum you crank a line around to pull on something. There's a glossary of sailing terms in the back of this book). I think that's all I learned, but it was a start.

Most of all, as tropical depression number one approached, I began to realize that I was doing something people dream about.

"Harrr! We'll make a sailorman of you yet," a voice (one I would later hear with increasing frequency) barked in my ear for the very first time. "Aye, that we will."

I thought I saw a glimpse of a graying gentleman in a British royal navy uniform duck down the companionway.

Despite any hallucinations that might have taken place, it was apparent that I had the opportunity of a lifetime. I was in a position to spit in the eye of danger. Though if I had done it in that wind, it would have blown back and smacked me in the face. Not that I had courage where others did not, rather I was at a junction of circumstance and opportunity. No one, save my own brother, would have taken the responsibility and burden of dragging the piece of baggage I was to the middle of the Atlantic Ocean. I would not do it today, and I am ever surprised and grateful that he did it then.

When tropical depression number one did arrive, it didn't take it long to wear out its welcome. According to Doug, we experienced between a force 7 or 8 on the Beaufort scale.

Force 7: Winds are from 28–33 knots and are near gale strength. The seas build to around 14 feet and can be described as large waves with some breakers that have foam blown down their sides in the manner of an overflowing glass of beer.

Force 8: Winds range from 34–40 knots and are of gale force. Moderately high waves have edges breaking into heavy spray. Waves are generally 18 feet in height, and foam is blown downwind as if someone had sneezed into a glass of beer.

Raise the Sails

Now you need to understand that an 18–foot high wave looks like a mountain to a Georgia boy who has never been to sea. The waves approached us from somewhere between the beam of the boat and its bow. *Windswept* would rise up what seemed a lot higher than 18 feet, and then rock back to starboard as the wave exited our port hindquarter. One time as a wave peaked beneath us, I peered over the side. I can pretty much swear I saw a little cabin with a smoking chimney and livestock in the valley below. I was certain that any second Heidi would run out the front door and yodel.

Doug assures me that all my descriptions of wind and wave are backwards. Please also understand that he claims to have actually heard Heidi.

Before the depression arrived we had hardly seen the sun for two days. Now we had scattered rain, big seas, heavy clouds, howling wind and queasy stomachs. It's a pure wonder more people don't take up this sport. I mean what other activity can you do in this weather? It would likely as not ruin a golf game. Try to slide into second base in these conditions and next stop would be the left field wall. Tennis, forget it. If you were out with your little buddies playing for keepsies, you'd probably take your marbles and go home.

The next morning our depression was over, or at least it had gone off to brighten someone else's day. Around 12:30, I spotted Bermuda. Everyone on the trip except Doug has claimed to be the first to see our destination, but since this is my story I am claiming that honor.

It really doesn't matter who saw Bermuda first because we each received a gift on that sail. "Cannonball" was the only person ever to see a pizza delivery boat five hundred miles into the Atlantic. Charlie Hardin, after numerous false starts, finally made it to Bermuda. Captain Doogie got to take the helm of his boat through Town Cut into St. Georges Harbor. And me? My gift was best of all, because when I stepped off *Windswept* onto the customs dock in Bermuda, I had my sea legs.

Chapter 4: *Selection Process*

When I get interested in something I have an overwhelming urge to learn all there is to know about the subject. And I am generally insistent that this process be completed in about three days. I'm sure this comes from a genetic makeup that leans toward incredibly short attention spans. That seems right enough, since my whole family is that way. Well, half of it at least. The males in my family have suffered symptoms of ADD long before the disorder was discovered and given a name. Combine that with a decided propensity for procrastination, and you get a recipe for an individual in a hurry, going nowhere.

I'm sure that's why everyone met my decision to buy my own sailboat with boundless enthusiasm. Take for instance the grand announcement I made at a restaurant near the docks in St Georges, Bermuda. We were sitting outside near the government docks attacking a late lunch. If I stood up tall, I could see Doug's boat, *Windswept* bobbing in the water, still rafted among a tangle of sailboats and lines adjacent to the Government dock.

"Well, I've come to a decision," I said, making certain that I paused just long enough for the anticipation of my announcement to build. "I've decided to buy a boat."

"Yeah, right," Doug said. He successfully hooded his enthusiasm amidst burger and fries.

"You gonna sail it in the tub with your rubber ducky?" Charlie asked. He always was the supportive type.

"No, I'm thinking of sailing it here—alone." A cold chill darted between my shoulder blades as a picture of this flashed in my mind.

"The needle on the BS meter is bouncing off the right side of the dial." I think it was Cannonball who said this.

"Come on guys, I'm serious." My good spirits are hard to dampen, especially when I have such a well-considered plan.

"Hey," the Cannonball said, "I know where a good pizza delivery boat might work."

God bless Warren, I told you he was a great guy. I'd known him far less time than my other shipmates, yet here he was doing his best to be supportive.

"Thanks, bunkmate," I said. It requires a highly developed talent for self-control not to turn criminal at times like this. "Good to know somebody's in my court. These other guys are perfecting their jackass skills."

"Come on, Bro!" Doug was possibly on the brink of experiencing a Covey sort of paradigm shift. "We were all on perpetual alert for the last week—scared you were going to jump off the boat out of sheer boredom. Now, we hear this buy a boat talk. I mean it's not like you're thinking straight. Have you been drinking?"

I thought, you pompous little—better nix that, after all, we are related by birth. I said, "I'm thinking fifty thousand. What kind of boat can I get that might make a trip like this for fifty grand?"

"A used one." Doug and Charlie said this in unison, which was rapidly followed by high fives over my head. "An old used one!" These guys were on a roll.

"I'm thinking a new forty footer." I said.

The idea of a new forty footer must have been a little overwhelming even to me because I almost spewed my sailorman drink from twitching nostrils. When I sat my glass down, it failed to make full contact with the table and shattered on the patio floor.

"The BS meter just exploded!" It was the Cannonball, that time I caught him.

Male bonding, there's nothing like it.

McGarvey's, October

Doug and I are at the Annapolis boat show; I think it's officially 'The United States Sailboat Show'. Anyway, same discussion, different gathering place. I had just dragged my brother around the Annapolis city docks looking at boats. Well, that's hardly true—the dragging part—any sailor not in heaven here is a power boater in disguise. Our original idea was to look at boats that I could afford. After less than an hour, we expanded our quest to those boats I could pay for. It didn't take long and we were on drool patrol. We really did try our best to keep anything from dripping from our lips onto the cabin soles of the Aldens, Hinckleys, and other died-and-gone-to-heaven boats we visited.

"You know, Doug a hundred twenty thousand is not that much for that Morgan 38."

"Too bad for you, Sid," Doug had the biggest smile I had ever seen, "I think you might wind up a boat owner yet. Because, son, that is some serious boat show fever I'm hearing."

"You like that center cockpit honey?" I was referring to the boat, not my brother or some brunette at the bar.

"Let's do a little more research. It might be time for you to see Cabo Rico."

Money, when you are in the throes of rapture, takes on a decided lack of significance. Somewhere between Cabo Rico and Valiant, I realized what boat shoppers around the world have come to understand.

I only needed a down payment!

Over the course of that afternoon, I learned that financing a boat was easier than buying a car from your local everybody-rides dealership. I mean, every thirty feet or so there was a booth full of lenders offering to make deals on the spot. Not that I wasn't skeptical, mind you. Had I not purchased several houses—all on credit? A house, as you may know, is considered reasonably good security for a loan. You can't move it without being extremely obvious and only then after securing the necessary permits and clearances. So the lender is pretty certain that their collateral will be where they left it, should they ever find it necessary to institute plan B. Despite having the stay-put guarantee of an asset that historically goes up in value, I have never been even seriously considered for such a loan without subjecting myself to a personal inspection that stops just short of proctology.

However, here I was decked out in shorts and T-shirt, and lender after lender assured me that all I needed was twenty percent down and a history free of skip-chase activity in the last five years. OK, they all agreed, three years was long enough. Keep in mind this is an asset that historically decreases in value and can be moved oceans away at the owner's whim. Naturally, I smelled a rat and began to really look under the tables they had set up dockside and behind their display curtains.

Finally, when one lender caught me rifling through his literature box, he asked, "Just what is it you keep looking for?"

"There's got to be a proctoscope here somewhere," I said.

Armed with the certain knowledge that financing was the least of my worries and having read enough of Tristan Jones and *Cruising World* articles to become an overnight expert, I began my quest in earnest. From Sail Expo in Atlantic City, to Miami and Ft. Lauderdale, I plied the boat shows. I read all the books available on the subject of sailboats. All this was well before I developed the personal sailboat theme song that I mentioned earlier.

The fact was my life had no theme. Personality had joined common sense on an ill-timed sabbatical. My marriage had been pronounced in critical condition by more than one well wisher and certified health professional. A business that I had worked for years to build was in the Critical Care Unit. The bowl that held my life was on perpetual flush and guess whose hand was on the lever.

All things considered this was a perfect time for my mother to die. The strongest person ever to be in my life was dead at eighty-one. On the day of her eightieth birthday she had undergone bypass surgery and almost immediately looked more like sixty-five than her true age. It wasn't that I depended on my mother, it was the knowledge that I could that I missed then and today.

Where do you turn when you are a middle-aged orphan with an ailing business and a marriage washed up on a rocky shore? You do what I did—find and buy a boat you can neither afford nor sail, and then embrace that midlife crisis!

I bring this up here to give you a sense of my mental condition. Apart from the hunt for the *Silk Purse*, I had lost enthusiasm for life. The prospect that I might lie down for the eternal dirt nap was not something that frightened me. This attitude shouldn't surprise you. Haven't I already explained the peculiar legacy shared by those in my family named Sidney? An Irish poet once wrote words defining death as the point in our lives where we can no longer muster enthusiasm for the masterpiece we will begin tomorrow. By this definition my search for the perfect sailboat became my only barrier to an early grave.

I warned you right at the beginning about these tangents.

Like I said, I became a permanent fixture at the boat shows. I had even read, from stem to stern, *Desirable and Undesirable Characteristics of Offshore Yachts*, by the Technical Committee of the Cruising Club of America, W.W. Norton & Company, 1987. This is a wonderfully comprehensive source for more than almost anyone who wants to know about serious sailboats. I could quote the positive range of stability for half the sailboats sold in the U.S.A. I made a list of my own desirable characteristics.

List of Desirable Characteristics

1. **Stability**: There has been a lot written and said about stability, but to me it meant resistance to heeling and ultimately resistance to capsizing. Few people want to voyage on a tender boat that drops a rail in the water

at the first sign of a blow, and no one looks forward to capsizing at sea.

2. **Strength of Construction:** I had zero intention of buying a poorly made boat. I would be putting my life in her care as I sailed the globe. True enough, but judging from the dirt-nap statement I just made, I think pride in my decision was the key factor. I wanted a bulletproof hull, an integral hull and keel and a well-protected rudder. I would have no part of a hull to deck joint that had screws in it; bolted only, please. There are many other crucial areas of construction, but if these were done without compromise, I would be on the right track.

3. **Seakindliness:** To me this means can a boat handle rough weather and heavy seas with a minimum of discomfort for the poor folks on board. I equated this with a heavily ballasted boat with moderate to heavy displacement and a long keel beneath the waterline.

4. **Big Boy Friendly:** I haven't told you yet that I have grown larger than the average man. This was achieved through a dedicated training regimen both in the weight room and the dining room. I really didn't want a little skinny boat. This fact would cause me to rule out several wonderful boats.

5. **Moderate Draft:** Anyone who wishes to spend time in the Bahamas, the Georgia–Carolina Low Country, Florida, or most of the islands needs a boat that floats in skinny water. I set for myself an absolute limit of six feet with a true desire for five. This again points to a long keel under the waterline. In this case, the long side is measured on the horizontal rather than the vertical.

6. **Livability**: *See* Big Boy Friendly. In addition to workable, well thought out space, I wanted a bunk I could actually get in with a minimum of body contortions. There should also be sea berths usable on every point of sail (don't confuse this with 'point of sale', which is where you give them the money for your boat).
7. **Value**: Here I don't mean cheap; there's no such thing as cheap. I wanted a boat that was likely to hold its value over time. Some of these things depreciate faster than a fuchsia and gold luxury car. Others hold their value well.
8. **Turn Around and Sigh**: My boat needed to make me turn around on the dock, gaze at her, and sigh every time I left her. I wanted a boat I could really love. We can get into what this says about the rest of my life later. I warn you though; it is much easier to love a good boat than a lot of good people.

Chapter 5: *Labor Pains*

Largo, Florida
March 1994

I made a right turn off Ulmerton onto Wild Acres Road. My decision was about eighty percent made that I would go with the Caliber 38. It was well constructed and I liked the layout. There were some things that I wasn't nuts about, but I couldn't even afford this boat. In my mind, there was no reason to pay the extra thousands of dollars for the Island Packet 38. So why even go to the Packet factory? Answer: boat fever, I had a temperature of a hundred and two, my pulse was racing like it used to, and I was probably addle-brained as a result.

I parked the car, went inside, and filled out the paper work where I promised not to sue if something fell on my head and killed me. After a short wait I met a young fellow by the name of Will Dittmer who showed another wannabe and me around the several buildings that comprised the factory. We saw how all the teak was matched for grain conformity for each boat. We watched as they worked with resin and glass to form the bulletproof hull of a 35. He showed me the difference between the new hull design on the 35 and the Island Packet's original design. He pointed out the recent open ocean races that this new hull design had won. This all sounded nice because few brag on the ossification factor of their boat, but the truth is no one who buys an Island Packet buys it to race. Maybe the Caribbean 1500 or Newport to Bermuda might be in their plans, but not around the buoys club racing.

Will explained the reason for using glass spheres to core and lighten the deck and cabin top and why this was structurally better than resin impregnated balsa. When we saw the way the chain plates became an integral part of the hull, I realized how truly fortunate I was not to have my checkbook with me.

Another thing I realized was that the 35 model I saw had more room below decks than most forty footers. Maybe I would be happy with the 35. Can you see what's happening? That's right. It's a trick. A trick I worked on myself, but a trick nonetheless. You see there is something magical about a forty-footer. I can't well explain it even today, but manufacturers understand this. Every 38 foot boat I was looking at measured forty feet or slightly better when taped from stem to stern. If I could convince myself that Island Packet was the design that best filled my needs, then it would only be one more step to the really big boy friendly model.

"Well, any more questions?" Will turned to me, as the other wannabe climbed into his car. "Anything you'd like to see again?"

"Is there a 38 here I can look at?"

"I thought I mentioned that," Will said. "We stopped making the 38. We're into the 40 now. She's got the new hull design like the 35. I don't think we've got one close to completion, just shipped two yesterday."

I knew it right then. That was it. The hook was set. They would ask. What kind of boat do you have, Sid? I would answer Island Packet 40. Sometimes, I would make them drag the forty-foot part out of me in a false show of modesty.

I said, "What's the closest dealer to Atlanta?"

"Southern Yachtsman is in Marietta. How close is that?"

This was beginning to sound like a conspiracy. I had a Marietta address. That being the case, I was reasonably certain that the closest saltwater was near four hundred miles away.

Remember the term *big boy friendly*? Two weeks later, I signed a contract for a new Island Packet 40. I ordered her as hull 22, but it wasn't long before she became *Silk Purse*. This boat had the unstated yet obvious promise to be everything I had hoped to find, and so she was.

Back again in Largo Florida, I turned off Ulmerton onto Wild Acres Road. Today I would see the Island Packet 40 hull number 22 emerge from the womb. I could well imagine how a proud father might feel as it grew close to the time that he would witness the birth of his first child. My throat was parched dead dry, and my palms were sweating. I had a camera around my neck like a dang fool tourist, and I had to restrain myself from snapping off a roll of film before I got out of the parking lot. I was here to witness a birth, once Will Dittmer retrieved me from the waiting room.

"They're just about ready to pull your hull from the mold." Will stuck his head through the door and motioned for me to follow. "I was beginning to worry you wouldn't make it."

"I had to stop and get film for the camera." I held up my wife's Nikon 35mm. She had carefully instructed me on how to use it only the night before.

We double-timed through the factory. As we neared the delivery room, my palms were really sweating. My heart pounded out a snare drum beat against my rib cage. I should have brought a partner to help me with those Lamaze breathing exercises.

"Breathe, breathe," I could almost hear Bill Cosby's famous voice over the factory PA system coaching me, using that Lamaze Rhythm. "Push, push—breathe, breathe—push, push."

We passed through a large doorway covered with those hanging down plastic panels like you see at the car wash, and there was the mold. A giant pair of forceps was poised directly above. My heart picked up a quicker beat. I grabbed the Nikon and snapped off two quick pictures, one of my feet, the other of the ceiling.

"Push, push—breathe, breathe!"

A few minutes later and the doctors lifted her from the womb. She wasn't all that beautiful with no deck, no teak, and the rough edges from the mold sticking out all over. But I loved her on sight, much in the manner of a proud parent who knows their newborn to be the most beautiful

baby ever born. The truth is, to the rest of us, the poor thing looks a lot like Elmer Fudd.

I snapped photo after photo until I noticed that I had a new rhythm in my mind. It sounded a lot like.

Da-da-da-da, Da-da-da-da. Now, add the horns and my sailboat theme emerges. Thank you, Mr. Mancini.

Chapter 6: *A Beginning*

The first time I saw *Silk Purse* afloat was in a muddy water slip in Masonboro Boatyard, located near Wrightsville Beach, NC. She had made her way from Florida perched heavily on the back of a large tractor-trailer rig. A huge, black and yellow sign stretched across her backside had proclaimed to all drivers on the highways that a wide load was ahead. I had carefully timed my arrival at Masonboro Boatyard so that I would miss her arrival and subsequent unloading from the truck. This was accomplished by means of a large marine crane lifting her off the trailer and swinging her through the air.

Once she was splashed into the water and tied to a working dock, that same crane would raise her mast and then lower it through the deck, through the cabin, and finally step it atop her keel. For the sake of all concerned, I did not want to see this, much in the manner I didn't wish to be around when the first hole was cut through her to install necessary equipment. Some things are just too painful for a new parent to witness.

Raise the Sails

Masonboro Boatyard possessed a personality that if not totally unique, then at least rare among marinas. I had learned of this rather crude, but totally acceptable refuge for boat people while accompanying brother Doug on his boat for a much-needed bottom painting. It was his boat that was to get painted. If the Oakley boys eat their vegetables and bathe regularly, marine growth seldom fouls our bottoms.

The boatyard was right near his house and I would need his help learning to handle the boat. This was the primary reason I'd decided to take delivery a full six-and-a-half-hour drive away in NC. So it wasn't surprising to see him walking my boat's deck when I arrived.

I steeled myself against being the butt-end of another of his little jokes and climbed on board just as if I had done it a hundred times before. Finally, the day had come. I walked up her starboard side then down her port. I was genuinely impressed with how the ten thousand pounds of ballast held her decks so steady. I mean she didn't rock at all, even with my tonnage crawling around from side to side.

"Man," I said, "I can't believe how steady she is!" I ran to the starboard shrouds and swung outboard as far as possible while keeping my feet on her rail. "I mean she is hardly moving at all. Look at her sit there."

"Hate to tell you this Bro," Doug said. "She's aground."

Yeah, right. I'm thinking fool me once…

"She's floating in her slip, moron." I wasn't fooling around now; I was in full tilt aggressive mode. "I suppose they sat her down on a rail spike and knocked a hole in her bottom?"

Doug shook his head and smiled, and before I could berate him like he truly deserved, the wind shifted. So did *Silk Purse*. She listed about ten degrees to starboard and hung there steady as a rock. I dashed down the companionway, certain that there were large volumes of water gushing through the three-inch rail spike hole in her bottom. Naturally, everything was dust-bunny dry. I bolted back on deck eager to demonstrate my new boat owner savvy.

"Hey!" I shouted across two slips and half the parking lot to the yard foreman who happened to be walking by. From the corner of my eye I saw Doug squint and turn his face away, already embarrassed at what I might say. "Hey, what did you guys do to my boat?"

Doug went forward and pretended to inspect the bow pulpit installation, which was as far from me as he could get without leaving the boat.

"What are you talking about?" The foreman lifted his hat and held it to shield his eyes.

"Hell, she's laying in the slip like she's sinking!" I wasn't about to take any crap this time.

"She's aground; it's almost low tide." He half turned then stopped. "We can move her to a deeper slip with the tide."

All right! So I don't actually need little brother to initiate the jackass effect. It evidently has an auto-engage mode.

Thus began two patterns that would prove persistent: running aground and overreacting. Thank God, I got past the overreaction.

Before being remodeled by Hurricane Fran, Masonboro was a funky shamble of a boatyard populated with transients and a permanent population that ran the gamut from the well-to-do all the way to the not-doing-too-well. In the slip on my port side was a semi-famous Houston trial lawyer on a beautiful Baba 40. To starboard I had the only sane people I remember, two marine biologists in the process of restoring their old Formosa ketch. A row of slips on the landside of the marina housed a group of dilapidated houseboats most of which I am certain would not have successfully crossed any body of water much larger than a child's three-ring pool.

Heading seaward was the "drunk dock" where I spent many a comfortable evening. The vessels here were mostly small, and less than half of them ever left their slips the better part of the year that I was in residence there. I remember one salty little sailboat that was so old no one in the marina knew its manufacturer or had ever seen its owner. That is probably the reason that the oysters felt so comfortable around it. You could tell they felt at home because they constructed an oyster bed that completely engulfed the prop, keel and half the rudder of what was once a sleek little boat. I never actually saw anyone harvesting oysters from that bed, but every now and then the rudder would get freed up enough to move an inch or two in one direction.

All of these vessels had two things in common: they served as a refuge for their owners, and they were all mainstream normal compared to the *Mole Hole*. The *Mole Hole* consisted of a rectangular ferro-cement hull that defied all attempts at determining bow from stern. A low wooden structure rose from the edges of the hull. Someone sometime ago had taken an old mop and painted the entire edifice a dapple gray. To the best of my recollection there were no windows or portals in the structure, at least none that I ever saw opened. Two large dorade vents together with stove and kerosene heater vents broke through the flat surface of the tarpapered deck. I could not look at it without thinking of the hideout used by Peter Pan and the lost boys to elude Captain Hook.

The *Mole Hole* could only be entered by way of a trapdoor hatch located in one of its corners. One of its corners is as specific as I can be. If a vessel has no discernable bow or stern, it becomes impossible to define port and starboard. She could neither be motored nor sailed. I don't believe she could be classified as a barge either, since all attempts to drag the *Mole Hole* from Masonboro Boatyard had ended in failure.

Though I received several invitations, I never went inside the *Mole Hole*. I used to sit and stare at it from the safety of my cockpit and imagine plunging down that entrance much like Alice chasing that dapper rabbit down its hole into Wonderland. Inside the *Mole Hole,* I was sure to find a universe where a Mad Hatter and a campy Queen of Hearts would hardly seem strange. On two occasions, fortified with the courage of Captain Morgan himself, I pulled open that trapdoor. Both times I was nearly overcome by the herbal smoke that gushed from the opening and hung over the *Mole Hole* like a shiitake cloud.

The *Mole Hole* was a mirror of the facilities at Masonboro, which were mostly broken. The toilets would flush OK, but more often than not you had to fill the tank with a bucket. The shower always worked, though if you flushed the toilet on a day it was in self-fill mode you scalded whoever was taking a shower. The one thing that I could always depend on was that the water coming from any of the spigots would have the richest combination of rotten eggs and natural gas aroma this side of spoiled underwear. And yeah, you guessed right; it tasted worse.

If this sounds like a coarse place, you would be correct, but it was not rude. The people and the place combined to create a nautical, homespun charm that translated itself into a wonderful refuge for broken people. That's why I fit in as well as I did. I was as broken as any there. And though I wouldn't admit it then, I was just as in need of refuge.

Perhaps it's time for you to meet the boat that became more than a refuge for me.

Silk Purse measured 41 feet 6 inches from stem to stern with a waterline of 34 feet. Her beam measured 12 feet 11 inches and seemed wider from inside. When loaded with fuel and supplies for cruising, she drew (depth of water required for flotation) 4 feet 8 inches and her mast rose 53 feet 8 inches above her designed waterline. This last statistic is an important one when deciding if you should attempt to sail under a bridge or not.

Silk Purse's Interior

When there was no wind *Silk Purse* was powered by a 50 horsepower Yanmar diesel that would push her along at about 7 knots in calm conditions. She carried 90 gallons of fuel, and if I motored her at a cruising speed of 6 knots the

Yanmar sipped fuel oil at about 0.6 gallons per hour. This gave her a range under power of 900 miles assuming all the fuel could be consumed. I would never attempt to motor a sailboat her maximum range for both safety and humanitarian reasons. In the case of *Silk Purse* her top speed becomes 8.5 + knots under sail.

Plus it's a lot cheaper (a word most sailors love) to travel powered by the wind rather than diesel fumes. Nor can the personality of a sailing vessel be appreciated with the engine running, only when we raise the sails. Another thing happens when you raise the sails; your range becomes infinity.

Her displacement was around 22,800 pounds. Fuel, water, supplies, and sailors brought her up to well over 27,000 pounds. This means even at 2 knots speed *Silk Purse* approaching a dock had considerable momentum. You don't simply reach an arm out and stop her. A considerable amount of intuitive ciphering is required each time she is docked or taken from a berth. Since her mass is constant, only decreasing her speed can reduce her momentum. Occasionally wind and current conditions make it possible to maneuver a sailboat too slowly, but slow, or better, near dead slow is a good practice.

Lesson: Raise the sails and our range becomes infinity.

Chapter 7: *Whistling in the Dark*

I was not the victim of a misspent youth. By age ten I had a paper route delivering the *Grit Newspaper*. I have always had a job. I can remember the day after my sixteenth birthday sitting in conference with my mother. We had all our cash on the kitchen table and both our bank account records opened in a desperate attempt to find enough money to buy two new tires for the 1959 Plymouth that she had inherited at her father's death. This wasn't to be my car; it was the only car. It needed tires; mother needed a way to work. We counted all our resources and determined that after I got paid Saturday, we would still be short.

My father wasn't available to contribute to the conversation or the new tire fund. Having lost another bout with Ancient Age *("If you can find a better bourbon, buy it.")*, he had succumbed to the irresistible call of the booze snooze.

I wish that I could say that it was uncommon for me to come home and find him in this state, but the truth is it was more times true than not. Neither my brother Doug, nor I, ever brought a friend home after school. The booze snooze experience was too embarrassing to share.

On the one occasion that I did bring someone home, we were just going to duck in the house and get something.

I was a high school sophomore and brought my first ever one true love by our little triplex apartment to pick up the $3.75 that was hidden in my sock drawer so we could go to the movie that night. I remember how beautiful she looked that day. Her blonde hair fell like spun silk to the shoulders of the little *Villager* sailor style blouse that together with the smallest hint of an early spring blush made her cute almost beyond my ability to endure it.

I eased the front door closed behind us, gave her the shhh sign, and crept past the closed door to my parent's bedroom. The bear was in there snoring away. Once past Senior's cave, I tiptoed to the bedroom I shared with brother Doug. We couldn't have been in the house a total of two minutes when I heard my father push open his bedroom door and grunt something at my love.

Sidney Senior staggered out of his bedroom in his ever-dingy Hanes grippies. I'm willing to wager that had Michael Jordan ever seen this sight he would have sold Fruit of the Loom.

He glared at my poor girlfriend as she covered her dropped open jaw with her hands, and said, "What the Hell's wrong with you?" He half belched then banged his toe on the coffee table. "Shit a nail!"

Senior continued toward the bathroom, pushed the door half-shut, and began to relieve himself. From the sound of it, he generated a pretty good head of foam in the toilet. My girl and I didn't wait for him to parade back through the living room and resume his booze snooze. She had seen enough, and I had had enough.

"Looks like another pair of retreads," Mom said and pinched her brow between thumb and forefinger. "We can only stretch things so far." She put on as good a face for me as she could. "You know just because things are tough now doesn't mean you'll have to spend your life like this."

When I was a young kid I was sentenced to do time in Augusta, Georgia, for what must have been a pretty horrific crime. We lived right across the street from the Richmond County jail, and after a few months I knew some of the deputies a bit, most of the trustees pretty well, and a few of the Saturday night hookers by name. However, when I close my eyes and picture those times today, it is not these characters that I see. Instead I see Osma.

My mother loved me and my brother beyond all else in her life. My father tried to love us, but at sometime in his life he had given his heart to Ancient Age. Having one devoted parent and one alcoholic parent is not unusual.

Having a friend like Osma was remarkable. The story in circulation at the time was that his mother dropped him on his head when he was a baby, but today I suspect a pregnancy or delivery problem for making Osma like he was.

Osma was a good man, but a strange man. He had a body chiseled from granite with blacksmith's arms and stone hard legs. At the time, he was considered slow or retarded. Today I remember him as simple: simple not just of mind, but of principle also. A thing was right, or it was wrong. You dealt with people kindly or not at all. You loved Jesus, or you did not. Osma loved his Lord Jesus about as much as anyone I have ever known, and together with my mother, he taught me to love him as well.

In those days it was the custom of all Baptist and most Methodist churches to hold a weeklong revival each summer. For one glorious week the church would have meeting every night. Services generally began on Sunday or Monday night and reached a crescendo that following Saturday.

Even though he was nearing forty, the only thing Osma drove was his bicycle, and in the summertime he rode it to revivals. Every night, or often enough to make it seem that way, he was off to some church to praise God and sing to Jesus. On some of his shorter junkets, I peddled my Huffy right behind him.

Wednesday or Friday nights were generally my favorites because that's when the singing would be the loudest. One night after singing about the 'little church in the wildwood' and our 'home in Gloryland' followed by a rousing chorus of 'doodle Lord' we had the obligatory altar call.

I remember well that we were half through the third verse of *Just as I am* and no one, not a soul, had come to the altar to meet the Lord.

"Oh God, touch someone's heart tonight!" The preacher raised his hands toward heaven in supplication. "Show us your saving power!"

Somewhere toward the beginning of the next verse I found my ten-year-old backside standing in the aisle between the rows of pews. Osma tried to catch me, but I was away, gliding toward God. People reached out with encouragement. They began to applaud.

More than once I heard someone say, "Well, if he can do it, I can do it."

When I arrived at the altar I turned and saw a half dozen people behind me. Halfway through the next verse I remember being surrounded by happy people—some grinned, others cried. It seemed like a quarter of the congregation crowded around the altar and pinched my cheek, mussed my hair, or thanked me for leading the way.

"Oh, Glory! You really started something here tonight!" The preacher pumped my hand. "You picked a great place to find the Lord."

I didn't tell the good reverend that I had discovered Jesus' whereabouts sometime ago at an earlier revival. Nor did I mention my puzzlement at a savior who seemed continuously lost himself. I was shy even back then.

Osma parked his hulking shoulders beside the minister and stood hat in hand. "He don't know what he's doing, Preacher." Osma shook his head and took my hand. "Come on here, Sid." He tugged me back toward our pew and turned back to the reverend. "He don't know what he's doing, preacher."

Osma was right. I really didn't mean to join the Faith Baptist Church that evening. I thought I was standing up for Jesus—just like the song instructed.

It wasn't long until my father at last found a job in Milledgeville, Georgia, and our sentence in Augusta was over. As our Plymouth Cranbrook pulled away from the Fenwick Street curb and headed to our new town, the only person there to wave goodbye was Osma.

In Milledgeville, I spent a huge portion of my life within the shadow of the First Methodist Church. Most who knew me then thought I would surely become a minister. I might have continued that path, but over the next year God became most noticeable to me by his absence.

Raise the Sails

I remember the exact moment I realized God was missing in action. It was Sunday evening and my seventeenth birthday was near. I was sitting in the choir loft while Reverend Charles Middlebrooks concluded his sermon. I don't remember what the minister was saying, only that I no longer believed it. I saw no evidence of any god, let alone the God of love as he had been introduced to me. God was AWOL. Where was he? Maybe he was on a booze snooze, I didn't know.

The next several years brought little change in the outward direction of my life. I finished college, got a good job. I stayed out of jail, worked hard, and prospered.

When Judi and I married, I think now that I thought then that I had it made. My wife was beautiful, enthusiastic, fun loving, and exciting. The next twenty years became my misspent adulthood, trying to live the childhood I had lost. My life mirrored the pattern of so many in my generation, who after protesting the Vietnam War and racism, and then drumming Nixon out of office, gave up the good fight for the good life. I was whistling in the dark.

I didn't cry when my father died, not the night it happened, or at the funeral, not even in private moments. I remember thinking I should. Possibly, I wanted the release of tears. The last time more than a stray tear or two washed down my cheek was in junior high, when I had to agree to put Trouble, my long-tailed cocker spaniel, down for the big dirt nap.

Between then and today there has been only the one time. Please don't label me a cynic or some sort of tough guy. I can be moved to the point my eyes overflow by the most obvious cinema trick, a good song that brings a memory to life, or even the AT&T commercial encouraging me to "reach out and touch someone." But scream into a pillow, gut wrenching type tears just don't happen.

The day that Judi told me we should, for both our sakes, get a divorce was the worst of my life. I had felt it coming. I knew I deserved it. Perhaps that's why I cried uncontrollably.

We sat on the patio in our backyard. Both of us had nearly worked ourselves to death trying to transform that plot of middle America from tract-home-suburban into something that was ours. The thought struck me that this was all there was to show for almost twenty years, and my misery deepened. I remember looking down at the growing stream of tears canyoning its way through dust, resolidified candle wax, and the remnants of burnt matches remaining on the glass top of our patio table from last night's meal. My shoulders spasmed, and I remember desperately wanting something to strangle.

At that moment the phone rang. When the answering machine picked up, I heard my mother's voice telling me that Virginia, the mother of my best friend through high school, college, and tomorrow had just died. I loved Virginia for all she was and all she had been to me. I thought of my friend, Bobby, how I needed to be there for him, but the truth was I couldn't be there for anyone. My despair became absolutely unbearable, so unbearable that I pushed Virginia's death from my mind. The next day, possibly the next hour, I didn't recall learning of her death. It would be over a year's time before I would remember that she was dead. Yeah, I know, sick puppy.

My reaction surprised Judi and astonished me. We had all the anger symptoms you read about. I delivered the snide comments; she glowered in disgust. I had escape fantasies;

she dreamed of being a vibrant and independent woman. She moved into the guestroom; I celebrated my newfound space.

Writing about that time in my life all but makes me physically ill. Like a lot of couples, we seemed almost perfect at first. I wanted to marry Judi two months after meeting her. She was the type of person I had dreamed about, and on some level been in love with, since my freshman year in college. She was the strong, independent woman that I had always wanted. We just didn't meet until I was twenty-eight years old.

I can say with some degree of honesty that it was a rare occasion that I allowed myself to know we were in real trouble. Most of the time I simply thought we weren't getting along. My life was in trouble, but what I didn't know was that Judi was in crisis. My greatest sin in our relationship was not the arguments, not the things said that still ring in my ears today, and not the ill will I often felt toward this woman I had loved before I knew her. My greatest sin was that I waltzed by her every day oblivious to how much she hurt and how hard she tried not to show it. I was whistling in the dark.

"Come on. Come on. You know what to do."

Enough about Judi, if you thought I was about to tell her story, you're in for a disappointment. The point is that *Silk Purse* and learning to sail her were the only positive things in my life. I was a results-oriented, wicked capitalist with a penchant for the party life, but the current results my life was producing were of no value. My mind had to be kept busy, entertained, or at least partially anesthetized because there was little substance beneath the constant activity or distraction. I fancied myself an amateur philosopher whose opinions were exceptionally well thought out. In the light of a new perspective, I can now see that my philosophy would not stand up to inspection beyond that which you might expect from a radio talk show.

The pages on the calendar kept turning, and Judi and I stayed together in an economic arrangement that cost us both far more than we saved. Finally, on the day we vacated our just-sold house, she and I went our separate ways. Still married, but separate. We would get divorced. We talked about it. We agreed to it. We even worked out a property settlement.

Chapter 8: *You Can't Learn It From a Book*

Had I but known the difficulty I was to experience on *Silk Purse's* maiden voyage, believe me I would never have let Billy Gardner in the marina with that video camera.

The sun winked at us as it ducked behind the only cloud in the pale Carolina sky that promised a perfect day for our first adventure. Poor *Silk Purse,* her first voyage was not to be down to the Caribbean, to the Florida Keys, or even along the coast to Charleston, but two miles up the ICW to my brother's house. We were determined to have a proper coming out party, no matter how out of character such an event might be. We even sent out invitations:

You are cordially invited to attend
The Commissioning Celebration
for the Sailing Yacht

Silk Purse

At the residence of
Kathy & Doug Oakley
6422 Shinnwood Road
Wilmington, NC 28409
At Six O'clock PM on August 20, 1994
Sid Oakley
Regrets: 910-555-2354

THE BOAT'S READY, COME DRINK SOME BEER!

I was so wrapped up in this boat that I'm sure you would have received an invitation had your address been available. Maybe you saw one anyway. It got a bit out of hand. I found them being used as coasters in bars and taped above urinals. On occasion, lewdly dressed women asked me if working girls were welcome. It promised to be the social event of the year. It was a good thing that living in Atlanta I didn't know too many people in the Wilmington area. As it was, the *Silk Purse* Commissioning Party was a little more rambunctious than Doug's wife was accustomed to. It wasn't meant to be, but like I said, things got out of hand.

But what sort of commissioning party would there be without the guest of honor? I had to get *Silk Purse* to Doug's house. This should not have been a major undertaking, since we're talking about traveling two miles up the ICW. The more immediate problem for me was getting her out of Masonboro Boatyard.

Like a lot of sailboats, the Island Packet 40 engine controls are on a single lever, conveniently located on the right hand side of the pedestal (that's the stand rising from the deck where the wheel and compass are). It's easy to work. When the lever is positioned straight up, the engine idles with the transmission in neutral. Push the lever forward and the transmission shifts to forward and off we go. The further forward you push the lever the more fuel goes to the engine and the faster the boat goes. The same thing goes for reverse only backwards. Sounds simple enough, right? Even a product of the Georgia public schools should be able to master the technique. What I didn't tell you was, there is a little red button at the base of the lever, right where it hooks onto the pedestal. If you push it in, the transmission stays in neutral no matter how far you pull back the throttle lever or push it forward the engine just runs faster in neutral.

On her maiden voyage the *Silk Purse* had on board me, a.k.a. Captain Useless, my wife Judi, Doug, and Trey (you'll hear more about him later) with the Gardner family acting as film crew. Two minutes before castoff I was a nervous wreck. I actually noticed my voice trembling, my hands shaking. I don't believe that during all the days and weeks that I would spend aboard *Silk Purse* I was ever as nervous (as opposed to scared which comes later) as when it came time to back her out of the slip that first time.

Our first attempt was thwarted before it really began. When I put her in reverse and pulled back on the throttle, we started sort of backward, but soon sprang gently forward toward the piling. It wasn't long before we noticed that my port bowline was still attached to the dock. Maybe some of those big sport fishermen powerboats have big enough engines to drag the dock along with them, but sailboats do not.

"I'll get the line," Trey said. To his credit he was still trying not to laugh. "Bow is free, try her again."

Raise the Sails

I pulled the throttle backward, and as the diesel revved up, I looked over my shoulder at the boats behind me. It immediately became clear that during the night someone had moved that entire dock of boats a lot closer to me than they were the day before. Turns out that I was prematurely worried; the boat wasn't going anywhere. I throttled the engine up to about 1500 RPM and looked backward in anticipation, but nothing happened.

"Sid, the tide is getting low," Doug said. "I think she's just a little bit stuck in the mud. Give her some power and we'll try and rock her side to side. Once we're out of the slip you should be OK."

I romped down on the lever. Doug and Trey took positions holding onto the shrouds (see glossary) on opposite sides of the boat. They hung as far outboard as possible and used a seesaw motion to get her rocking side to side.

"We'll wallow out a trough here in no time," Trey yelled, as he leaned far out to starboard.

It wasn't long before thirty thousand pounds of sailboat, crew, and gear rocking side to side through about a sixty-degree angle began to make waves inside the marina. Soon the boats tied up on either side of me began to rock in their slips as well, causing a chain reaction through the marina. This, of course, brought more than one puzzled or hung-over boater topside of their vessel to see what was going on. Several of them pointed at me and hollered out some words that I was certain were encouragement until I saw a couple of those well-known international hand signals aimed my way.

"Sid, Sid!" Billy Gardner finally got my attention and held his video camera aloft. This is all great footage, but if you're rocking like that you're not aground."

"He's right," Doug said.

I'm not sure, but I think that was what Doug said because by now the diesel was so loud I couldn't hear anything. It was right then that I knew beyond a doubt what was wrong. With some deliberation, I eased the throttle back forward to drop the RPM level of the engine down below 1000. Praying nobody would notice, I slipped my hand down the lever toward its base. Sure enough, when I realized we were tied to the dock, I had pushed in that cursed red button. The entire exercise had been attempted in neutral.

"I don't believe it!" Trey pointed at my hand trying to slither back to the wheel. "He had the thing in neutral." He reached for the dock. "I'm getting off this thing, we're not gonna make it to your house, Doug."

On our third attempt we managed to back relatively straight out of the slip. We even turned the stern slightly to starboard, which made our exit from Masonboro a lot easier. Someday if you ever own a single-screw, full keel sailboat, you will understand how truly lucky I was in managing this maneuver. In general, when you put these things in reverse they tend to go more or less sideways and to port, except when they do something else.

Our bow cleared the slip, and I continued to ease the boat aft so that we would be able to exit the yacht basin. Remember, how I told you it looked like those boats behind me had been moved closer? Well, now they were getting really close.

"Put it in forward, Sid," Doug said trying not to sound nervous.

I pushed the lever forward and *Silk Purse* continued backward. I increased the RPM's and she continued aft. Doug jumped across the cockpit and released the red button.

"Leave that button alone!" He shook his head and looked at Trey in complete bewilderment. He had obviously forgotten that me being right here right now was almost as much his fault as mine.

For those of you wondering, the transmission held up well when slammed into forward at 2500 RPM. However, it is not a recommended procedure. We managed to get out of the boatyard without further incident. We turned north up the ICW toward Doug's house. As we approached each waterway marker, I had to basically rethink the entire reasoning for the green marker being on my right. That would make the red one on my right. No left!

The Captain Doogie manor was located up a small canal that connected with the ICW. The canal's size relationship to the waterway was similar to a sidewalk's to a main highway. I could barely keep *Silk Purse* between the ICW markers. Doug's canal? No way.

"Hey Bro," I said with as casual an air as possible. "You do realize that you gotta take this thing up your canal?"

"I was afraid of that." He didn't look a lot more confident than I felt. "Well, let's see how she handles."

Doug took the wheel and made a couple of figure eights and tight turns. A minute later we were dead slow ahead navigating his canal.

The following week I maneuvered *Silk Purse* out of the marina and into open ocean at least once a day. I would sail on a beam reach in whatever direction I could and then turn and sail back to the inlet. Once back inside protected waters it was practice anchor at least once then put her in the slip. I loved everything except docking the boat.

For the absolute novice like I was, Island Packets are the best and worst boats to learn to handle around the docks. The good part is once you learn to handle this style boat the others seem easy. The difficulty is due in part to the high freeboard the design presents to the wind. However, the real culprit is the full keel that gives them such great seakeeping qualities makes her less nimble than some of the skinny, girly fin boats around. When I first began looking at this design of boat I was warned that I would be unable to maneuver in tight quarters at all. Maneuvering around the docks did not prove impossible, but it did present a problem for the uninitiated, which I certainly was.

One time in particular Doug and I brought the boat in and I began my turn into the slip too late. We had gone over this possibility numerous times when we were sitting on the dock or over lunch. Over and over little brother had told me that if I got in a tight situation—get out. This means that rather than trying to salvage a blown maneuver, take the boat out of the tight quarters and bring her back in. That is, start over. You probably learned enough on the blown attempt to get it right the next time. But, remember, the title of this chapter is "You Can't Learn It From a Book".

Today the wind was positioned so that it would push us into the slip once we were aligned properly. If, however, you get the boat beam to this wind, you can find yourself docked across the stern of your neighbor's boat before you know it. Trust me on this.

By October, it seemed time to take *Silk Purse* on her first real trip. We would sail her from Wrightsville Beach area to the little hamlet of Beaufort, NC, "Gateway to the Caribbean", and a community considerably influenced by sailing. The town got its nickname because beginning in late fall many sailboats from northern ports head down the ditch (sailor slang for ICW: Intracoastal Waterway) until they reach

Beaufort, then head offshore toward sunshine and the Caribbean.

Maybe you remember Beaufort was also our departure port for the Bermuda trip that started this whole business in the first place. This time rather than sneaking up on the town from the rear by way of the ICW, we planned a full frontal approach. We would come in right through the channel that we had exited on the way to Bermuda. Somehow this seemed appropriate.

You need to know two things if you are going to get along in Beaufort, NC. First, it is pronounced in the French/Southern manner that is, **Boe** fert. Second, do not confuse it with Beaufort, SC, which sounds like Buford as in T. Prosser from *Smokey and the Bandit*. The South Carolina version is a delightful Low Country town with its own affinity for sailboats.

One time Doug and I were stopped in the South Carolina version of Beaufort and pulled into a fast food joint to grab a quick breakfast sandwich. He had been telling me about how the people of South Carolina didn't even know how to pronounce the names of their own cities, as evidenced by their pronunciation of Beaufort. I assumed the more enlightened position that the people of the area didn't wish to sound phony French then add a 'fert ending to their town name. Either that or they said "Boefert" as well. To settle the point, Doug went to the counter and told the young man working there that we were having an argument that had led to a wager as to how to pronounce the name of this place where we were. Could he pronounce it slowly for us to settle the bet? I have to tell you that guy looked at Doug and me like we were both nuts and said, very slowly.

"BURRR – GERRR – KINGGGGG"

Back to the trip: I arrived at the boat after a six-hour twenty-nine minute record setting drive from Atlanta. I was a bit tired, but fired up to leave that afternoon rather than the next morning. Doug was already on the boat basically ready to go.

By this time, Doug was spending a lot of nights aboard *Silk Purse*. He and his wife were planning to settle their differences like mature adults—in court. I, on the other hand, had convinced myself that if I procrastinated long enough, my own marital problems would go away.

Within an hour of my arrival, we had exited Masonboro Boatyard and were approaching the inlet through which we would escape to the freedom of the Atlantic.

When I think of the sea, freedom is my overwhelming impression, both freedom to and freedom from. I never had the fear of the open ocean that a lot of sailors must overcome before they can enjoy even coastal cruising. I think this is because I learned there rather than in the relative safety of Lake Catch-a-fungus somewhere inland. I have a well-deserved, healthy respect for the sea, but little real fear. I have heard the sea described as cruel, but I would take issue with that term as being too human. She can be unpredictable and relentless in her manner and ever diligent to punish a lack of preparation or any procrastination. But cruel? No, that is too much like us for anything as majestic as an ocean.

Once through Masonboro Inlet, we picked up a WNW wind that put us on a nice broad reach to Beaufort. Our plan was to sail all afternoon and through the night to Cape Lookout Bight where we could anchor before dawn with the ghosts of such pirates as Blackbeard, Bonnet, and Moody. The late afternoon sun was still warm and comforting on my back while the 12–15 knots of apparent wind felt cool on my left cheek. It was less than a quarter hour before my troubles at home and at work were far from my mind and the steady immune-to-aspirin ache at the base of my skull departed for the first time since I had left *Silk Purse* the previous weekend.

A couple of hours later we sailed a course of about 70° magnetic and the boat knifed through easy three-foot seas at a little over seven knots. At this rate we would make the Bight in time to get plenty of rest before heading into Beaufort the next morning.

Darkness crept up on us and we were able to see the lights of Wrightsville Beach in our wake. They faded to a dull loom then disappeared as the black of night fell on us like Dracula's cloak. I slipped into a sweater and punched Doug indicating my willingness to take another turn at the wheel. It was just then that the compass light went out.

I felt a little surge of panic, but beat it down easy enough secure in the knowledge that we had a number of flashlights on board plus a one million candle power search light suitable for conning in a UFO.

"That's the first thing on this boat not perfect," Doug said.

"Yeah," I said. "I was beginning to get a restoration of faith in American business that I lost back—"

"We're not about to hear that Captain Marvel story again, are we?"

"Bite me."

"It's hard enough steering a course by compass in the light," Doug said. "It's near impossible in the dark. Try and find a star to steer by."

I looked, and the problem was not finding a star but finding just one. The pitch darkness at sea made the stars seem to multiply into Carl Sagan type numbers. It wasn't long before I had the boat heading in all sorts of wrong directions. I'd fall off downwind until the sails luffed then overcorrect and head to windward until they luffed again.

Doug handed me a flashlight. "Get her back on course. I think she'll steer herself better than this."

Sure enough once I had her on course Doug balanced the sail trim and she held her course with a minimum of interference from me. We sailed along like this with me checking the compass every two minutes, and Doug telling me to relax. I found myself making minor course adjustments every third or fourth check. All went well until the wind died.

The wind dropped to zero. We cranked the diesel then rolled up the headsail.

No boat will steer itself when it's motoring, not without an autopilot. And mine just went below to take a nap. I was on deck alone—in charge. I checked my watch: 2200.

It would be about eight hours to daylight and I was already so sleepy I couldn't hold my head up. As it drooped closer and closer to my chest, my body would suddenly jerk back to startled awareness in that reflex action most have experienced when our bodies demanded a comatose state at a time when sleep was not an option. After the third time my head recoiled off its breastbone pillow, it finally crystallized in my mind that I was in charge. Me. I stopped worrying about how long I could resist the urge to summon Doug from his rest and resolved that come what may I would captain my own vessel. Moments became hours and *Silk Purse* and I became acquainted on a level I had not thought possible. She didn't need a firm hand, but a decisive one.

Could this be a clue to the key to restart my life? It seemed to make more sense than the whisky bottle, but then new ideas are often difficult to sell. At the moment it seemed enough to pilot my vessel.

Sometime later a tiny red light winked in the distance almost straight ahead. What was it? Another boat? Maybe it was some sort of marker or a lighted tower on the distant shore ahead. A quick check of the compass confirmed we were on a course of 72° magnetic—perfect. It winked again, and my star became a red light located just port of my bow.

A couple of minutes later, my light had vanished. I flashed a light on the compass. No wonder I couldn't see the light, I was heading dead southeast—a perfect course to the Cape Verde Islands. This was a little too ambitious a destination for a captain having trouble maintaining contact with the east coast of North America.

I turned us back on course to the Bight, and almost immediately saw a quick spot of red flash then vanish. I waited, and there it was again—two quick flashes and out.

It didn't seem to be moving, and since it was blinking regularly every five seconds, I knew it wasn't a boat. Best of all, if I put the bow slightly to the right of the light I could see it blinking to port. I was right on course. Several spot checks over the next hour confirmed that we were still on course, still steering toward the light. I couldn't go to sleep, but I could relax some. *Blink-blink* 1, 2, 3, 4, 5 *Blink-blink*. I counted and steered. Each time I did a compass check we were right on course. I found after sometime that it had a pretty good rhythm.

I felt a gust of air on my left cheek as *Silk Purse* heeled hard to starboard. The wind was back. I released the main sheet some and we came a little upright. Once the main was properly eased, I unfurled the jib and the boat came to life. I doused the engine and serenity replaced the rattle of the diesel.

I checked my watch 0320, about time to wake Doug and go below for a nap myself. As I stood to fetch my autopilot, I noticed the light had turned bright and had gotten a lot bigger. Before I could figure that out, the buoy was ten feet off my port bow. We were going to hit sure as hell. I jerked the wheel hard to starboard and *Silk Purse* lurched to the right with enough force to send Doug, who was stepping through the companionway, stumbling across the cockpit. The buoy passed us to port close enough to spit on.

Five minutes earlier the light appeared dim and seemed quite distant. That night I got a first hand demonstration of how a light at sea always seems distant until you are right on it.

"Hard to believe we've got the entire Atlantic, and we almost hit that thing." I said.

"Why wouldn't you hit it?" Doug yawned at me. "You've been steering toward it all night."

I hate it when he's right.

We managed to approach the entrance to Lookout Bight without further incident. This was due primarily to the fact that I was asleep in the cockpit most of the way.

I checked the chart; all seemed in order. The buoy that marked the entrance to the bight was blinking red every six seconds just as the chart showed it would. I could do the chart reading fairly well since that was something I could learn from a book.

Doug steered us into the Bight leaving the red buoy to our right. We headed straight for the lighthouse that stands a little over 150 feet high; its bright light swept the anchorage every fifteen seconds just like the chart said. We passed the green marker to port and anchored in about twenty feet of water. I opened a bottle of Mondavi. We toasted our success at 0500 and promptly dropped off to sleep.

The next morning Doug found me already up and in the cockpit studying the chart.

"You're up early."

"Easy to be early when you're with Rip Van Winkle."

Doug put a finger on the chart right in the center of the Bight. "We're right here."

"I'm trying to figure out which buoy we almost hit last night."

Doug started counting up time and figuring speed and distance by the multiple finger abacus. Ciphering ability is a family trait.

"We couldn't have been more than ten miles from here. What were the characteristics?"

"Two quick red flashes every five seconds by my count."

He grabbed the chart. It didn't take him long to get the answer. "You almost collided with the Beaufort sea buoy. "It's sitting out in the water about a quarter mile past an old buddy of yours—Red Four."

"And you thought I couldn't navigate," I said.

"Bite me."

Sibling bonding is a wonderful thing.

Lesson: Simple accomplishments can be fulfilling if they are a stretch achievement.

Chapter 9: *Cutting the cord*

In the weeks that followed her first trip, *Silk Purse* took Doug and me on a number of trips to Beaufort. Depending on the wind direction, we sometimes sailed to Beaufort or occasionally motored up the ICW. Once the wind shifted hard on the nose for a return trip as well, and we motored back down the ditch to Wrightsville Beach. It really didn't matter to me what our route was, since I needed the experience in either case. On the ocean leg, I learned coastal navigation, open water navigation and comfort with the sea. In the ditch, I learned to navigate the ICW buoys, which are different from the channel buoys, except when they are the same.

The most important lesson I learned navigating the ICW and gunk holes between Beaufort and Wrightsville Beach was that running the boat aground was not the end of the world. We found every shoal marked or unmarked between Beaufort and Masonboro Boatyard and spent the night on a couple of them. I learned from experience and stories from other sailors (notice how I am now thinking of myself as a sailor) one of the several axioms of sailing. Axiom: There are three types of sailors: those aground, those who have been aground, those who will be aground, and those who never go anywhere. The corollary for this axiom states: There are three types of people, those who can count and those who can't.

After each trip Doug would ask what I had learned. We would go over this with a fervor that neither of us had for other forms of higher learning. After we covered what I had learned, he would without fail tell me what he had learned on the trip. This was a practice that I can truthfully say I maintained until the day I left *Silk Purse* for the last time. I never once took her out of the slip or hauled in her anchor that I didn't learn something.

As the weekends came and went, the drive between Atlanta and the boat began to get old. The speeding tickets in South Carolina got especially old.

My skills were growing. According to Doug they were growing a lot faster than I realized. Still, I had not ventured from the slip at Masonboro alone. There is a world of difference between taking out a fishing boat with single or twin engines and handling a fifteen-ton sailboat with a big keel and a small motor. I brought occasional guests from Atlanta to day sail and spend the weekend on *Silk Purse*. We would take her out into the Atlantic and sail up and down the coast then back to the slip with only minor incident. Each one would marvel at the way I had learned to handle the boat, but this was faint praise to my ears. After all, they knew less about boating than I did.

One Sunday night when I had made up an excuse to stay in the area an extra day or two, Doug and I found ourselves perched at the bar of a favorite watering hole. We had come there for the expressed purpose of admiring the bartender's backside. After a couple of beers the subject turned to my progress in the art of sailing.

"How did Ken like sailing?" Doug asked referring to a friend who had come up for the weekend.

"He enjoyed it, but I think he was glad when we got her back to the slip." I said, remembering Ken's green complexion and early departure for Atlanta.

"Did he get sick?"

"A little, bored is more like it." I shook my head and thought of Judi, my estranged wife back in Atlanta. She liked her boat trips short as well. "This isn't for everybody."

"Let me ask you, how much help was Ken out there?"

"Help?" I thought a second. "None."

"Docking the boat, how much help was he then."

By way of reply, I gave him my confused basset hound look.

"Docking," he said. "Tell me, how much did he help you then?"

"Well uh," I stammered. Even I could see where this was going.

"Say it."

"Less than none. I had to pay so much attention to Ken I almost hit the dock."

"And you would have been…." He wasn't going to let this go until I actually said it.

"OK, I would have been better off docking the boat alone."

"Now all I have to do is get you to believe it." He raised his hand in the Richard Nixon victory sign that for us meant 'two more'.

Raise the Sails

As hard as Doug tried to get me to embrace the area, the North Carolina Coast didn't feel like home. I always felt like a visitor there. A more self-inquisitive person might have realized that maybe his feelings were due to unfinished business at home and office. A person less skilled in the art of self-deception might have realized that I would never feel at home in North Carolina as long as my heart was in the state of denial.

I decided it was time to move the boat to the Georgia coast. It didn't take much of a scouting expedition to determine that *Silk Purse* would make her new home at St. Simons Island berthed at Golden Isles Marina. It was soon to become home for her owner as well.

I would take her as far as Charleston, SC, then on to St. Simons the following week. Leaving on a Thursday morning, we would sail all that night and could expect to arrive in Charleston early afternoon on Friday. This should not have been a problem. It was about double the trip to Beaufort, and Doug and I had made that leg a number of times.

My problem was that two weeks before I was to leave for Charleston, Doug told me he couldn't make the trip. I pretended that this didn't bother me, when, in actuality I could imagine how a young bird must feel when his parents start pushing him from the nest. I *knew* I could do it; I just didn't *feel* I could do it. I had the skill; I just lacked the confidence. So I did the only thing I knew to do. I invited others to share in my ineptitude.

Crew for Sid's first voyage as a real captain:
Sam Barazzone: The Island Packet dealer that sold me *Silk Purse* who was an accomplished sailor, but inexpe-

rienced offshore. This would be a learning experience for him as well.

Mike Bramble: Experienced gunkholer and offshore sailor, Mike and Doug brought *Windswept* back from Bermuda. It was the return leg of my voyage that started all this. He is also the author of the sailor's song that begins this book.

Billy Gardner: Billy taught Doug to sail so I knew he could be captain by default if Captain Sid went into panic mode. And yes, he was the leader of the Gardner film crew who still had copies of Captain Useless backing *Silk Purse* out of the slip for the first time.

Right away Billy and Mike decided that they would share watches, and leave Sam and me to handle things on our watch. This would force me to be in charge at least half the time. I was nervous about the trip, but not afraid. I knew we were not likely to get into too much trouble on such a short hop, even if it was a long leap for me.

I backed out of the Masonboro slip for the last time. To my great pleasure the boat and I performed that maneuver with aplomb. We turned north toward the inlet and Doug brought *Whisper* alongside with a couple of friends to take pictures of my exit from the Wilmington area. We motored through the inlet together and both of us set sail. We had about twelve knots of wind on a gray rainy day in June. It wasn't long before Doug, *Whisper*, and the Masonboro inlet were out of sight.

The wind was blowing from the south, which meant that once we were far enough offshore to be out of any danger of grounding, we needed to roll up the genoa (headsail) and unfurl the Yanmar (diesel) if we were going to turn toward

Charleston. If you look at a chart of the East Coast, you'll notice how the shoreline slopes back west rather sharply all the way to the Georgia/Florida border. This is called the Georgia Bight and is one reason that coastal Georgia has been over one hundred years without a hurricane. Most storms tend to approach the area from the southeast, then veer north and go over the roof of Doug's house where it sits at the very base of the North Carolina barrier Islands. Anyway, by heading hard south we could make some progress towards Charleston while increasing our distance offshore.

More importantly, we needed to avoid Frying Pan Shoals. Again, if you look at a chart covering the extreme southern portion of North Carolina, the shoal is easy to see. However, when sailing along in almost complete darkness, avoiding the shoal becomes infinitely more important than finding it. It was imperative that we navigate around it. As I write this, I have my NOAA chart 11536, Approaches to Cape Fear River spread out beside me and the points of position that we made that night are still penciled in. Looking back at the route I picked for us, I see an adequate albeit simple piece of navigation. Doug was right: I had learned better than I realized.

From the chart it is easy to see how the shoal got its name. It makes a recognizable replica of a frying pan handle extending SSE from Bald Head Island. This group of shoals is one of the reasons that the waters off the North Carolina coast are referred to as the Graveyard of the Atlantic.

Today the shoal is well marked and we decided to sail south far enough east to clear buoy Red "2FP" by at least a mile. Once we had passed that marker to starboard we could safely turn west toward Charleston.

Log Entries:

1445 Killed Yanmar, sailing under full main and 130 genoa, wind 14 and backed to ESE

    Speed 7, course 186° M (magnetic) N34° 04.7' / W 77° 43.4'

1545 wind building to 20+ double-reefed main, full genoa, C 194M, S 8

1645 wind continues to build 25+ double reef main and staysail. C 194

2045 Red 2FP flashing red 6 sec to starboard, confirmed on GPS, altered course to

250°M double-reef main full genoa, S 6.6, heading for Charleston

The seas built to 8 feet and we sailed a comfortable broad reach with the wind and seas approaching from our port quarter. There were differing opinions as to the degree of comfort on board as Silk *Purse* stepped over the seas, rising and tipping to starboard with each wave exactly like she was designed to do. This motion would rock me to sleep if left alone more than a minute or two. However, Sam's stomach had begun to roll before darkness settled over us. When he got smacked in the face by a flying fish for the third time in less than an hour, I began to worry that he might throw himself overboard to escape his nausea. Sometime before dawn his cheeks lost that 'bout-to-hurl-green in favor of his normal rose complexion, and we thought he might survive. I kept offering him boiled eggs and sardines or a fantastic beef burgundy I made prior to our departure, but he declined.

Later that morning the wind dropped and the seas calmed to a perfect little rise and fall. After breakfast we popped the cruising chute (cruising chute: a large lightweight sail used for generally downwind sailing in modest to light air). I had just bought it from one of those secondhand sail purveyors you see in the back of the sailing magazines. I had only used it a couple of times and I'd been salivating to raise it on this trip.

We set the cruising chute and bold stripes of bright red, yellow, orange, and white flashed in the sunlight. Hey, don't blame me for the color combination; I said I bought it on the cheap. *Silk Purse* took to her new wind engine with a passion, and we drove across the Atlantic at better than seven knots.

Two hours and fifteen nautical miles later the South Carolina coast became a small hill on the horizon. At least I hoped it was the South Carolina coast, as irrational fears of a major navigational mistake raced through my mind. I went over the possibilities very carefully and determined that it was either the South Carolina coast right near Charleston, or we were in the Twilight Zone. I hadn't heard Rod Sterling's voice, but I remembered that back on the Bermuda run I hadn't seen Cannonball's pizza delivery boat either.

We sailed on, with crew in bliss and captain on 'worry watch'; until Billy Gardner lowered the binoculars from his eyes and turned to me.

"Pretty good job, Captain Sid. That's the north jetty at Charleston Harbor right there." He stretched his arm out straight ahead of us. "I'd recognize that anytime."

I realize that it's not like I had found Fiji using a toy sextant, but my chest about exploded with pride. I tried my best to act as though it was already the common occurrence that later such an accomplishment would become.

"Go ahead, Sid," Mike said. "It's okay to smile."

We continued on course until the wind died. Then we doused the chute and dropped the main. As we approached Red 8 we turned into the Charleston harbor Channel, and continued between the jetties. A few minutes later and Fort Sumter was on our left. Since the Yankees and the Rebels had long since surrendered the fort to the tourists, we entered Charleston Harbor unmolested by cannon fire.

It was here after passing Fort Sumter that I began seriously worrying about docking the boat. I had worried a bit about docking all the way down from Masonboro Inlet. When the wind was blowing 25+ knots, it was only in the back of my mind. When the chute was up, I worried about the docks. When we dropped the chute, I was worrying about docking.

I went below and turned on the VHF radio. "Charleston City Marina, Charleston City Marina, *Silk Purse*."

"Vessel calling Charleston City Marina, please go to 6–8, over."

"6–8," I acknowledged.

Normal VHF procedure is to hail your party on channel 16, and then pick a working channel for your conversation.

"*Silk Purse* on channel 68."

"How can I help you, Captain?"

"Yeah, we'll be needing a slip till Sunday. We are a 40–foot sailboat, drawing five feet. Can you accommodate?"

"Right enough, Captain. I'll have to put you on the face dock right beside the seawall. You'll enter through the cut and turn starboard and snug up behind that little trawler already on the dock."

"That's a roger, *Silk Purse*, standing by on 1–6." So we had a place for the weekend.

It was still early afternoon, and across the harbor the city awaited us. We cruised past the battery and eyeballed the old gun emplacements. Next came White Point where almost three hundred years earlier the "Gentleman Pirate", Stede

Bonnet, had been hanged and buried below the tide line. I hoped our prop wash didn't disturb his bones.

We continued up the Ashley River and turned into the City Marina. The current was running about four knots on our stern, making stopping in our space on the face dock without smacking the boat ahead a little ticklish. But we had gotten this far and we would get her stopped. I needn't have marred the last ninety minutes of my trip with worry. There on the dock stood my teacher and little brother, Captain Doogie, waiting to take my dock lines. The cord had been successfully cut, but the bond remained in tact.

The welcome to Charleston party had succumbed to an early death, and I took advantage of everyone's absence to catch a short nap. I awoke, and a little past three (1500 sailorman time), I reached into the fridge and came out with a bottle of Korbel Natural that we had been too tired to drink the night before.

"Don't do that, man." My buddy Trey had driven down to see if we would make it to Charleston alive. "We're about to get messed up."

"No," I said, "we can drink this and still act in a responsible manner."

"Oh, hell."

I should have listened to Trey. I awoke the next morning with a blacksmith pounding on an anvil inside my head. I rolled over on my side and managed to get one foot on the cabin sole before the pain in my lower back crippled me. I could understand the headache. I mean I'd worked hard enough for it the night before. But this low back thing was a bonus. I stumbled to the forward head and dumped a handful of Advil in my palm. I washed them down with a few gulps of water and noticed that my mouth tasted like someone nasty had washed their socks out in it. Yes sir, buddy, this single life could be good to you.

From experience, I knew that only the real thing would help with the taste. I braced my back with my left hand and used my right hand for balance as I made my way to the galley. I raised the lid on the fridge where, if there were a God, a Coca-Cola would be waiting to acid-wash the taste from my mouth. I popped the top off a Diet.

Ptsshh. Help was on the way.

"You sorry rascal." It was Trey crawling off the settee in the main salon. I hadn't even seen him. "I told you what would happen."

I grunted something that couldn't have been too pleasant and stumbled back to my bunk. Some hours later with my sins at least partially purged, I realized that I would live.

Since it was necessary for the boat to remain in the Charleston area while I worked accounts in Greenville and Spartanburg, SC, Trey and I needed to move *Silk Purse* to a slip in the Wild Dunes development. She needed to be moved there because a friend of a friend of Doug's was loaning the slip to us free of charge. At $42 plus tax a night to leave her at the public docks, the *Purse* would run up quite a tab for the wallet. That's how sailors are: cheap and generous.

I mentioned that on the way into the marina we had a four-knot current on our stern pushing us toward the other end of the boat basin and the row of boats tethered there. We had it again only this time it looked more like five knots. The marina was set up so that our only way out was to our rear. That meant we had to either back the hundred-fifty yards to the marina entrance or turn the boat and its full keel through the current until we were able to head out pointy end first.

Trey advised us to back out into the current and continue in reverse until we made the turning basin at the marina entrance. My thoughts were that since the boat liked to back to port anyway we could swing the stern out to port and then turn her nose into the current. This would allow us to motor out bow first. Trey suggested again that we back out. He was most forceful in his opinion, which I naturally ignored. I mean, hadn't I only two days before successfully navigated the Atlantic?

We tossed off our stern line and spring line. *Silk Purse's* stern swung out to port just as I'd envisioned. Trey released the bow and hopped on board. I hit her hard in reverse and sure enough the stern swung out so that the current struck our starboard beam. I kept her hard in reverse, but the stern refused to move further to our left. We were now heading dead sideways with the current toward the boats docked at the end of the marina some fifty feet away and closing. I hit reverse full throttle and she only picked up speed in the down-current and sideways direction.

This was the birth of the second term I would add to the sailing lexicon, "velocity athwartships". This of course is the speed that the boat makes good sideways and is a condition to be ever minimized. What was happening, I would later come to understand, was a combination of two things, both working against me. The rudder was heading down current, sideways to its design and therefore was completely ineffective. The prop now rotating in the direction we were heading acted like the paddlewheel on one of those Mississippi riverboats. The more I slammed the throttle down, the greater became our velocity athwartships. *Silk Purse* was heading beam first toward the docked boats and a genuine screw up.

"Put her in forward—hard!" Trey screamed as the bowsprit of a good-size Sea Ray drew dangerously close. "Spin the wheel over."

I did it, but too late. It didn't help.

From off the docks and off the boats a half dozen people boarded the Sea Ray and ran to her rescue. Trey caught the bow just as it slipped across my lifelines and threatened to T-bone my cabin top. He turned blue pressing, trying to hold us off the Sea Ray. Other hands assisted and slowly we moved forward across the bow of the powerboat. This process was repeated until we passed across the bows of a total of four additional sailboats, and we were finally able to turn into a vacant slip at the end of the dock.

After we gathered our breath Trey backed us out against the current. He spun her around in the turning basin where there was actually room for the maneuver and motored out of the marina. Trey wouldn't let me drive my own boat for the balance of our trip to Wild Dunes. I suppose I was in the penalty box.

I learned that lesson well. Well, sort of.

Chapter 10: *Going Solo*

It didn't take long for St. Simons Island to begin feeling like home. When I left North Carolina, my reputation as a screw up remained behind. Simply the fact that I sailed an Island Packet 40 lent me a degree of respectability that I had not enjoyed in the Masonboro sailing community. After all, the folks that sailed from St. Simons had missed my first attempt at leaving my slip. One night after an early dinner with some of my new acquaintances, I decided it was time to begin to live up to my new reputation.

I awoke the next morning with a sense of excitement. Today was the day! The sun was still struggling to vanquish the darkness beyond the golden grasses that comprised the salt marsh defining my western horizon. Already I'd listened to the NOAA weather reports that promised this would be a perfect day. Even the tides were cooperating. I would be able to leave on the ebb and return the following day on a flood tide. This meant that *Silk Purse* and I would have a relatively easy time leaving and returning to our slip. I scurried up the companionway and patted her cabin top. I knew she would not let me down; I hoped as much of myself. Today was the day she and I would cross St. Simons Sound and enter the Atlantic unsupervised. Solo, a cappella.

If you remember, the Georgia Bight is defined by the westerly bend of the coastline beginning in Florida from the south and the Carolinas from the north. The Atlantic bites deepest into the eastern coast at a point right near St. Simons Sound. This is one of the reasons that the tidal range of these waters is so large varying: from six to nine feet. Every six hours the water level either drops or rises six to nine feet. This causes a great flow of water laden with vital nutrients in and out of not only the Sound, but also the rivers and creeks that form the salt marshes, which make this area so picturesque.

The Georgia barrier islands, such as St. Simons, are commonly known as the Golden Isles. Their moniker comes from the golden-topped grasses that beckon in the coastal breeze and are home to a remarkable variety of wildlife. Microscopic crabs grow to number one jimmies in abundance. Shrimp and an endless variety of fish mingle with marsh hens, otters, and alligators to form a magnificent ecosystem. On a daily basis, several varieties of dolphin can be seen swimming through the rivers and sound harvesting their share of the bounty. It takes only a little imagination to send a cold chill of fear crawling up my back for the fate of our planet's food supply should our salt marshes ever vanish.

End of heartfelt, obligatory ecology tangent.

The flow of water borne nutrients makes the area a haven for barnacles. These crusty little devils attach themselves to almost any surface and wait for the movable feast that passes by them with each ebb and flow of nature's oldest cycle. One of the surfaces that seemed especially attractive to them was my ever-submerged propeller. Barnacles loved the polished bronze surface of *Silk Purse's* prop so well that every two weeks I was required to prepare for battle by donning mask and snorkel. Then, at slack tide and armed with a heavy-duty painter's spackle tool thingy, I climbed down her stern and scraped off the new crop of barnacles that had attached themselves to her prop. This was an absolute requirement if I was to even think of backing out against the sometimes six-knot current that flowed through my slip.

On the afternoon before my big day, the prop was especially encrusted. As I worked on the crust growing on the prop, scraped away barnacle particles filled the water around me. The current that carries the nutrients also churns the waters around the Golden Isles loading estuaries with lots of mud and silt. This required that I get exceptionally close to the prop to adequately clean it. I was just finishing when I felt a rough pinch against the back of my head. I jumped and, of course, banged my skull against the prop, which initiated a stream of underwater profanity. I felt around in my scalp—no bump, no gash. Determined to finish before the tide built, I went back to work. Pinch! I felt it again, this time accompanied by a sharp tug on my hair. What was it? Pinch. Bump. Pinch. I spun around my spackle-tool-thingy held out in my defense, my mouth full of brine, heart thumping like a captured bunny's.

There before me, big as a pizza, was a harmless sheep's head fish. It had followed the trail of barnacle bits, snapping them up all the way to the back of my head. The sheep's head makes a great meal, and somewhere I could hear the dinner bell ringing. However, before my thoughts of turning the table on my attacker crystallized in my prop-bashed cranium, she retreated into the dark cloak of brine. I later learned that this was a relatively common experience.

What wasn't common was my first true solo sail.

The NOAA forecast I mentioned before promised WSW winds blowing ten to fourteen. I would sail the less than thirty nautical miles from the St. Simons inlet through the St. Mary's inlet. Once through, I would turn south and anchor off the city docks at Fernandina, Florida. I realized that this was not an ocean passage, but for me it was a right of passage. To sail anywhere offshore without the assurance of someone more experienced to check my navigation and verify I was doing the right thing represented a large step toward the fulfillment of my dream to become a real sailor.

First, I had to get out of the slip at Golden Isles Marina with my dinghy (dink) in tow. I slid the dink from *Silk Purse's* bow and tied it on a short tether to her stern. The day before I had bought some of that special polypropylene rope that floats on the surface of the water. The idea was that if it's floating on the surface it won't get wrapped around the prop or shaft. When this happens you tend to look like what you feel like—a genuine, bonafide dope.

As the sailing gods would prescribe, the current was on my stern at a good four plus knots. The day before I had polished my prop to slick bronze, so I knew that I could power out. I had the dink positioned to prevent it from catching the dock on the way out and Chick, the dock master, had my bow and spring lines. I tossed off the stern line and powered her back at a little over 2000 RPM (red button out). *Silk Purse* began to move slowly backward. I brought her out with her stern pushing the dink out of the way. When we were well clear of the dock, I put her in forward, and we were free.

I turned beside the dock and waved at Chick who had no idea that this was my first solo. He waved casually back. A moment later he was shouting and pointing astern of me; I looked back and there, in full free float, was the dink. I could see the frayed end of the floating painter (dink towline) drifting lazily with the current. At least the boat and the dink were heading generally in the same direction.

I spun her around (expletive deleted) bow into the current and realized that with a little luck I could capture and again secure the dink. I adjusted my engine speed so that I had almost zero speed into the current. No need for panic, I would wait for the dink to come to me. I retrieved a boathook (telescoping metal pole with hook on one end) from a locker. Sure enough the dink soon bumped us on the nose then slid down the port side and I captured it. I tied the dink and hooked her to our stern with another line. This time I added a longer safety line, just in case.

I towed the dinghy well out into the sound, pleased that I'd resisted the urge to set it ablaze with the flare gun. All that remained was to turn our nose into the wind, set the autopilot, and raise the main. We (*Silk Purse* and I) were soon sailing with the engine off and serenity reigning supreme.

I continued through the Brunswick Harbor-Bar Channel until I passed green 1A to starboard, and then turned south to a course of 165M. The seas were calm in the lee of the Georgia coast and the boat became a piece of ice sliding over a mirrored surface. After adjusting the sails I was able to hand steer her with little effort, often not needing to touch the wheel at all for upwards of five minutes.

We continued generally south for a couple of hours before the wind began to die. In less than ten minutes time, my perfect wind had been replaced by total calm. The genoa swung on its halyard limp as a dishrag, and the main hung from the mast like half a pup tent. After half an hour the tide began to return to the Marshes of Glynn and the GPS told me we were drifting at about two knots toward Andrews Sound. Rumor spoke that this was a tricky entrance, and I didn't want to experience any tricks on my first sail alone.

I cranked the iron spinnaker (Yanmar a.k.a. diesel) and rolled up the genoa. Two minutes later we were motoring straight for St. Mary's Inlet still some fifteen miles ahead. Two hours later I was sailing hard into twenty–five knots of warm air from the southeast. The seas had built to eight feet and my little dink was being tossed about like a cork in a Maytag.

The water shallowed out to below thirty feet as I approached buoys 16A and 18 in the center of St, Mary's Channel. The waves began to bunch together and assume a squared shape. I checked the dink just in time to see it make a complete somersault. Actually, it was more like a one and a half with a twist because when the dink landed it was belly up and I was dragging it backwards. It was not designed to be towed like this and the chances of losing my transportation to shore seemed good. I rolled up the headsail and turned us into the wind with the diesel in gear and turning about 1200 RPM. I set the autopilot and began hauling the dink towards the stern. If I could get it close enough perhaps I could flip it back over and tow the cussed thing into harbor correctly.

I couldn't get it done. At least not with the poor leverage I would have sitting in the stern five feet above the dink. I opened the gate in the stern pulpit, unfolded the swim ladder and dropped it into the Atlantic. I tied a twenty-foot leader onto my harness tether and began backing down the swim ladder. *Silk Purse* hobby horsed on the waves as if she were trying to get my attention.

Halfway down the ladder, one more step and I would be knee deep in the Atlantic I heard a harsh voice rattling in my ear like pea gravel shaken in an empty Coke can.

"Just what in the Davy Jones do you think you are doing there, mister?" A strangely familiar voice boomed from *Silk Purse's* cockpit. "Get up here, boy!"

"Aye, Captain Oakley!" Instinctively I knew his name.

I climbed back up the ladder toward safety just in time to catch a glimpse of the Royal Navy uniform complete with tricorn hat disappearing down the companionway.

"Bugger that dink, sailor!" He shouted from below deck. "Are you out of rum?"

"Sir, no sir—behind the dinette table, sir!"

I would never learn why I found it necessary to conjure up Captain Oakley to set me straight, nor did I realize then that I would soon see him again. I'm just glad I listened to him. Well, that time anyway.

He was right, "Bugger the dink!"

Lesson: There are several in there; you can pick them out.

I continued through the St. Mary's Inlet, between the southern tip of Cumberland Island and the northern beach of Amelia Island pulling my dink upside-down and backwards. The bow wave in front of the dink was almost as large as the one at *Silk Purse's* bow, but she didn't seem embarrassed by her captain. I like to think she was glad he was still aboard, and not being drug belly-up in tandem with the dink.

I arrived at the Fernandina anchorage without further incident. We circled around the almost empty anchorage and

Raise the Sails

dropped the hook in about twelve feet of water. I let out enough chain and rode (anchor line) to accommodate the two more feet of water that the tide would bring. I began to contemplate dinner ashore when the dink once again grabbed my attention.

Astern of us she still floated upside-down. Rather than have someone claim it for salvage, I hauled it along my port side. She slid through the water with practically no effort at all now that we were no longer moving through eight-foot seas. However, the dink's inflated edges and stern board made a perfect seal with the water and thus all my attempts to right her were in vain. Each time I lifted, a partial vacuum would form, and I lacked the strength to break the seal. No problem. I attached the spare halyard to the tow ring on the dink and cranked it into the air with the winch. A moment later and she floated with no harm done astern of us like a proper little boat. I did resolve then to get a set of davits so it could hang off the stern out of the water and restrained from further circus maneuvers.

Less than an hour passed before a salty looking Albin trawler entered the anchorage. He circled around evidently watching his depth sounder until he was happy with the location. Instead of dropping an anchor he produced a leader and attached it to a piece of line that in turn was attached to one of the several white spherical floats that dotted the anchorage. I was not aware that there were any moorings in this anchorage. I had seen a number of floating white markers, but they were not mooring balls.

During his circling he came close enough for me to read the name from his stern. I decided to try and raise him on the radio.

"*Sea Daddy, Sea Daddy, Silk Purse* calling." I released the transmission button on my VHF and waited. "*Sea Daddy, Sea Daddy, Silk Purse.*"

"Yeah, *Silk Purse*," the radio squawked his reply. "Let's go 6-4."

"6-4." I twisted the tuning dial to channel 64. "*Silk Purse* on channel 6-4."

"Roger."

"I'm not trying to be a wise guy or anything." I wasn't the least bit comfortable with what I was going to say. "But sir, I believe you just tied up to a crab-pot marker."

"Man, I think I know a mooring ball when I see one." His reply was a little terse, even over the radio. "What kinda crap are you trying to pull? Calling somebody on the radio trying to make him look like a dang fool!"

I promised I would not have done that. I knew from recent experience that it was no fun to look the fool. I suppose he had no way of knowing that though. Besides, he didn't seem to need any assistance bringing off what had all the earmarks of a jackass maneuver. Possibly he was less aware than some concerning the ease with which King Neptune can transform one from gallant captain to braying ass.

"Don't call me again!" Terse, definitely terse.

"Sir I'm sorry, I –"

The radio screeched back at me; he was holding his mike button down. I turned off the radio and turned on Toni Braxton. I knew she'd get me back in a good mood.

That evening I motored to the dinghy dock. The town of Fernandina had a number of good and not so good bars and I was considering writing a book entitled *Bars, Dives, and Watering Holes on the Intracoastal Water Way*. This was to be a research trip. Carefully taken notes were required.

Raise the Sails

When I tied up to the dock there was only one other dink there. Across its stern I read *t/t Sea Daddy*. With any luck I would miss the owner during my research trip. I stopped at the marina office to pay my dinghy fee for tying to the dock. When I stepped into the cool air conditioning, a burly man with graying temples was leaning on the counter. He pulled out his wallet and pointed out the window toward his boat.

"How much for one night on the mooring out there?"

"For what?" The dock master looked up with a slack jaw and wide-open eyes.

"The mooring, how much for the mooring? Now I'm only staying here one night." His tone was emphatic. He wasn't about to be stuck for a two or three night fee. "How much? I'm only going to be here one night."

The dock master fixed him with a tight-jawed grin. "You won't even be here that long, unless you get out there and get an anchor down before that tide kicks up. There are no moorings out there. Best I can figure you're tied up to a crab pot."

I swear I didn't say a word, but I did near bite a hole in my lip to keep from it.

Lesson: Be careful. Sometimes you're not the dumbest one out there.

That evening I cut my research short and motored back to cook a piece of dolphin (the fish not Flipper) for dinner. I opened a bottle of chardonnay and ate topside with the Bimini top opened and the stars watching me watch them. Not in heaven, but in a pretty good spot.

The next morning I awoke when *Silk Purse* swung 180 degrees on her anchor announcing that the tide had turned. I went topside and noticed that I had left the swim ladder down all night. When I did pull it up, there were three beautiful blue crabs clamped onto the bottom rung of the ladder. I supposed even the local wildlife needed an occasional rest from the tidal currents. I introduced my guests to the human custom know as breakfast. I hope they enjoyed it as much as I did, though it seems unlikely.

I didn't bother with checking the weather report because I had already decided to take the waterway back. I had yet to make this trip, and I was anxious to see if it was as beautiful as I had heard.

I pulled up and secured the anchor, then put her in forward and we began our initial exploration of the inside passage between Fernandina, Florida and Golden Isles Marina. This is a journey of around 38 statute miles and should take about six hours via sailboat.

We began motoring north in the Amelia River with a southerly breeze. I popped the jib open and let the sail out until it luffed then trimmed it in a little more than was optimum in the hope that this would reduce the amount of sail handling required. Soon we passed Little Tiger Island and cut across Cumberland Sound putting the brickwork of Fort Clinch on our stern.

Silk Purse and I continued more or less in the channel past Kings Bay. On subsequent trips through the area, I saw up close and personal the big boomer submarines returning from and leaving for parts unknown. But today I had the deep-water channel all to myself as I approached the naval base.

The waterway between Fernandina and St. Simons is some of the most wonderful low country scenery in the world. Heading north from King's Bay the waterway becomes a dark river meandering through grasses and woodlands. I steered through a channel off to the right, which, if I read my chart correctly would be the Brickhill River. A mile or so further up stream there was still plenty of water and we worked our way along the serpent's back with Cumberland Island to our right and salt marsh to port. By now the sun was on its decline and the morning crab breakfast had dissipated.

When I rounded a bend and the river widened, the idea of rushing back to St. Simons for no particular purpose lost any urgency it had previously possessed. I would drop the hook here and have lunch. Afterwards, we would resume our journey, or maybe not.

An hour later we opted for not.

Lesson: When I was a small boy in Milledgeville, GA, we used to go to a place out from town about 10 miles toward Macon. It was called Peaceful Valley, and their motto was "if you're in a hurry, hurry on". Cruising under sail is most often like that.

Chapter 11: *Abaco Cruising*
April 1996

The early morning air was wet and thick with no-see-ums the day Charlie Hardin and I left for the Abacos. There was no wind and the bugs were brutal. Every time I wiped the moisture from my brow, I got a handful of black specs, each representing about a hundred bugs. They buzzed around our heads so that we were constantly inhaling them live through our noses only to spit them out dead from our mouths a moment later. We backed out of the slip knowing that our only relief would be on open water. Halfway into the sound, we both breathed a sigh of relief.

It was not the bugs of coastal Georgia that had made Charlie just a little shy about joining me on this trip. Not too long ago he had witnessed my absolute incompetence as a sailor on our trip to Bermuda. So I was not surprised to learn that Charlie had called Doug and Trey to get their opinion on his chances of seeing Abaco alive with me at the helm. I was pleased to learn that each of my mentors assured Charlie that we would most likely arrive in one piece. Eventually.

Raise the Sails

Abaco! The northernmost portion of the Bahamas and many say the most beautiful. I could already hear the Gully Roosters Band playing. *Let's go, go, go to Abaco!* I had been to the Abacos once before. I had flown into Marsh Harbor, met Trey and his wife, Jan, and then sailed as crew with them back to Florida. We had gone to Green Turtle Cay and partied with friends then did a serious transit back to Ft. Pierce, Florida. I was definitely ready to go, go to Abaco.

As we exited the Brunswick channel the wind was on our nose and in direct opposition to the exiting tide. This kicked up closely spaced box shaped waves that caused *Silk Purse* to hobbyhorse and pitch in a short, jerking motion. To help dampen our motion and since the wind was on our nose, we decided to raise the main. I went to the mast and connected the halyard, released the lazyjacks, then began to raise the main. Two good pulls and progress stopped.

"What's wrong," Charlie asked in a tone that told me he knew something was sure to screw up sooner or later.

"Not sure," I said, then looked aloft and saw the problem instantly. "The halyard is wrapped around the 'Blipper'".

A week or so before, Doug and I had installed the semi-famous Friddel Blipper passive radar reflector. Which, when viewed from the outside looks like a two-foot-long suppository bolted to the forward portion of the mast somewhere above the spreaders. When viewed by a ship's radar, it makes a small boat like *Silk Purse* appear to be a freighter. The idea is that anyone on duty is more likely to see a large blip on the radar screen and avoid running down the boat.

"That sorry Doug must have left the halyard wrapped around it last week when he bolted it on!" Last week I had given him the option of being cranked up the mast via the spare gib halyard or cranking me up.

"How can we get it lose?" Charlie looked aloft while hanging onto the shrouds for balance. "Let's toss a line over the spreaders and maybe we can pull it off that way."

"OK."

In principle this was a good idea. However, we could never toss a line thirty feet into the air without a weight on it, and anything hard was likely to chip our skulls or worse the gelcoat when it came crashing down on the deck. I tied a piece of light line to a small diving bag and put a baking potato in the bag. Now, we had a soft-weighted line.

Thus, began the Brunswick Channel offshore great potato toss.

I set the autopilot. Then Charlie and I took turns tossing the bag toward the spreaders. Our problem was that, in this chop, the deck was far from steady. Simply looking aloft was enough to tax our balancing skills. Add a stout throwing motion, and the exercise became almost as dangerous as it was ridiculous. After reducing our second potato to raw mush, it became obvious that another plan was called for.

"One of us has to go aloft," I got the bosun chair from below. "Crank me up, and I'll get it cleared." I wrapped one end of the spare jib halyard around a winch on the mast and handed Charlie a winch handle.

He looked at me like I had lost my mind. "You expect me to crank your wide-load butt up that mast?"

"Either that or I'll crank you up. It's…"

"I'd rather do that."

Charlie sat in the bosun chair, which consisted of a wooden seat wrapped with canvas that was brought up from the sides and across the back. The halyard was then threaded through two stainless O-rings and tied off. It made a relatively secure seat. The halyard ran from the bosun chair, to the top of the mast, through a block and back down to my winch. I cranked him about half way up and as the boat pitched forward, Charlie swung out toward the bow. When the next wave came, it lifted the bow and pitched Charlie back toward the center of the boat where he was reintroduced to the mast with a respectable smack. It became apparent that we would need a second line to prevent his swinging away from the mast. Once properly rigged, he was back down in about five minutes, job completed.

On our second attempt to raise the main, the halyard stalled after two pulls just like before. I looked aloft and there it was wrapped around the Blipper in identical fashion.

"What the hell?" I pointed aloft.

Charlie's comments were unprintable.

After Charlie's second trip up the mast, we realized that the halyard, if left with any slack, would be thrown forward as the boat pitched forward. When the boat rocked backward it snapped the halyard with just the proper 'English' that it wrapped the Blipper.

"Well," I said, "looks like it wasn't Doogie's fault after all."

"The hell it wasn't!" I looked at Charlie the confusion must have shown on my face.

"That's probably the only spot along the entire length of that mast where this could happen. I say he did it on purpose."

"Naaa." I shook my head. "He's not that smart."

Lesson: At sea, experience and preparation will generally trump enthusiasm. Some weeks later I realized that by attaching the spare halyard to the main halyard, I could easily dislodge the wrapped line with no going aloft or potato bashing required.

Because the Gulf Stream can flow north at three plus knots, it must be taken into account when plotting a course to the Bahamas from Georgia or elsewhere along the East Coast. To a sailboat moving at less than ten knots a three-knot set back becomes very significant. The normal sailboat route to the Abacos is to sail close to the Georgia and Florida coasts and inside the northbound current until you reach the Lake Worth Inlet at Palm Beach. You can then head east, cross the Gulf Stream and onto the Bahamas Bank, or do what most people do. You anchor or take a slip in a marina and wait until the weather is favorable for a Gulf Stream crossing.

When the wind blows with any real strength from the north, the opposing current of the Stream produces higher and rougher seas than normal. This condition is almost always uncomfortable and occasionally a bit dangerous.

Weather on our arrival was rough. Waves topped at 10-12 feet, but we were going to take a slip anyway. Our wives, Martha and Judi would be meeting us in Palm Beach, as would Doug on his boat. There were other boats that we planned to meet and form a sort of conga line across the Gulf Stream. Once in Bahamian waters we would morph into a flotilla party traveling through the Abacos.

We stayed in the Lake Worth area for two days then crossed to the Bahamas Bank over calm seas and without incident. That night we anchored *Silk Purse* along with Doug's newly acquired Shannon 38, *Whisper*, at Great Sail Cay. The following evening we dropped the hook in the Allans-Pensacola anchorage. When Trey dropped anchor about a hundred feet off my port beam, it was party time, and an evening of wholesome debauchery reigned supreme. Judi and

I were getting along better than might have been expected for a separated couple, though she and *Silk Purse* had not really warmed to one another.

The following evening, *Silk Purse* anchored near the government dock at Green Turtle Cay and Martha and Judi's spirits rose noticeably. There were restaurants here.

About midmorning, Charlie and Martha caught a water taxi to the airport then flew back to the States. In a few days, Sam (boat dealer) and Gwen Barazzone joined Judi and me. Each day they were with us we had a splendid time, but as it grew closer to time for them to leave, I became more and more apprehensive. Not simply because Judi would fly back to the U.S. with them, but because that would signal my next rite of passage. I was to sail *Silk Purse* back to St. Simons Island nonstop and solo. This was to be my first significant single-handed passage, and I was much more nervous than I let on.

I had no shortage of offers from sailors wanting to crew back with me, but I needed to do this. The folks back home at Golden Isles Marina were not aware that I was a rookie. Most of them thought me an accomplished sailor more because of the boat I had than because of the skills I exhibited. In my mind, it was time I lived up to my boat.

I waved good-bye to Judi, Gwen, and Sam. Before they had time to make it to the taxi stand, I had *Silk Purse* free of the dock at the Conch Inn Marina, and I was motoring through the huge anchorage of Marsh Harbor. It was my intention to meet up with Doug in Green Turtle Cay then sail with him and his crewman Billy Gardner (film crew from party and crew to Charleston) back to Allans-Pensacola. We would spend a quiet night there, then get an early start the next morning.

When I entered the anchorage at Allans-Pensacola, there was Trey's boat, *Tres Bien*. So much for the quiet evening.

Doug and Billy declined the invitation to a communal dinner, a last night's supper. I wasn't so sensible. Also, I was on my boat alone, and a dinner with Trey, Jan, and friends was appealing. We cooked a few pieces of fish and killed a few bottles of wine. When Trey suggested a prank on Doug and Billy, I figured that they deserved it. I got into Trey's dinghy and he handed me down a huge kitchen-sized bag of garbage that he had been forced to hold on to for several days. It had been his thought that he would have to keep it until he arrived in Florida, but now there was an alternate solution to the problem.

We paddled the dink to Doug's starboard side. When we were close enough, Trey caught the side of the boat and we set the bag of garbage on Doug's bow. We continued past the galley where Billy and Doug were cleaning up after their meal and we overheard them talking.

"That was a good decision not to go over for dinner," Doug said. "We'll be glad in the morning."

"What time you want to go?" Billy took a dish from Doug and wiped it dry. "Still 0600?"

"Yeah, old Bro oughta have a pretty foggy head about then."

They both thought that was funny. So did I. In fact, Trey was forced to cover my face with a life jacket to keep me from giving us away.

"We'll have him too sick for the offshore challenge and kick his butt." Doug held up his hand for a high five. Smack! Their hands met overhead.

"Don't you think the two of us can sail faster than him?"

As we drifted away I saw Billy looking at Doug as if the possibility of Silk Purse and me out sailing them had never occurred to him until this moment. We drifted too far down wind for me to hear Doug's reply, but I'd bet he was pretty confident. And why not? I'd never been in a real sailboat race in my life and they were seasoned veterans.

The next morning I was awake before dawn. I had listened to the cruisers net broadcast the day before and heard a very favorable weather report for the next several days. But I had the VHF on anyway so I could coordinate with Doug on our departure.

"*Silk Purse, Silk Purse—Whisper.*" I heard Doug's voice scratch from the radio speaker.

"Yeah, Doug." I answered.

"Did you have anything to do with this?"

"What?"

"What? This…this bag of crap on my bow, that's what." He was trying hard to sound tough, but I knew his only real problem with the prank was he had not pulled it on one of us. "Well I'm —"

I began making static sounds accompanied by bumping the mike key. "I can't hear you Bro—radio trouble." I had to hold my privates to keep from peeing my pants.

"Radio trouble, my butt."

I went topsides and saw that Trey had already left the anchorage.

"Hey Doug," it was Trey over the radio. "What was that I saw on your bow this morning?"

It really was one of those times you had to be there. I will tell you this, and then no more trash talk. A week later Doug sent a UPS package to Trey's home. Guess what was in it?

I had my anchor up, main up, and was motor sailing behind Doug on a northwesterly course toward Moraine Cay. A half-mile southeast of Moraine we turned due north. The water depth went from 12 feet to 60 feet then fell off the range of my depth sounder within another half mile.

Doug was a couple of miles ahead of me, and I was sailing along dragging an artificial lure off a hand line about sixty feet behind me. Just as I hit 60 feet of water I got a strike and pulled a little three-pound Spanish mackerel on board. I invited him to stay for lunch. I tossed the lure back in the water and hadn't dragged it 50 feet when it was hit hard by something. I towed my catch about a hundred yards and began to pull it in toward the boat with a laborious hand over hand motion. I guess it was within twenty feet of my stern when a triangular fin streaked through the water. In an instant, a shark snapped up what I had judged to be a small to moderate sized barracuda. The line jerked free from my hand, snapped tight and kept going. Just as well because I had no intention of asking the shark to dinner.

Log Entry: 0820 position: 27° 06.0` N / 77° 46.2` W, Course: 330° M Speed 7.5 knots. Seas confused and rough, only 3-5 Doug & Billy 1-2 miles ahead

By 1020 *Silk Purse* had closed the distance on *Whisper* enough that I could see Doug and Billy scurrying around on deck trimming sails and trying different sail combinations. Yeah, they were about to let a rookie pass them. I had the autopilot steering while Billy was at *Whisper's* wheel coaxing every erg of energy possible from her sails. I went forward to sit on the bow rail and watched as we slowly but relentlessly closed the distance on *Whisper*. By 1100 we passed them and the radio came to life.

"Damn it Sid, your sails aren't even trimmed."

I pressed the transmit button. "Well, we're trying to keep it low key over here."

"I got a key for you."

Truth of the matter is I had him by about three feet in waterline and almost twenty years of boat design evolution. Even I couldn't screw up that advantage.

Log Entry: 1740 Doug out of sight, Caught a fine wind, S 8+, C 324° M

I sailed that night over rough but not large seas. Speed over the bottom (as read by GPS) occasionally reached 9.5 knots with the aid of the Gulf Stream current. This was about a knot and a half lift over my speed through the water.

I warmed up some spiced beans and ate them wrapped in a couple of tortillas and washed them down with two Miller Lites. They didn't taste particularly great, but they were less intoxicating. Drunkenness is no virtue when sailing alone.

Darkness arrived and I was ready for it. We were well out to sea. Though it was unlikely that I might hit another boat, this was my greatest fear and danger. A well-found sailboat is exceptionally able to weather most storms with just a little help from her skipper, but she is a poor risk if challenging even a small freighter. Still, I would have two nights of this single-handing and I figured that I should get some sleep in the bank in case the weather deteriorated. At 2045 I recorded my position speed and course, dismissed the idea of a third lite beer in favor of a bottle of water, and retired to the cockpit. I stretched out on the seat and tucked a throw-cushion under my head for a pillow. The seas were less than four feet, but rougher than a cob, causing *Silk Purse* to take on a bouncing, jerking motion. One minute later, I was all but tossed onto the cockpit deck for the first time. After several failed experiments with positions and body angles that should have braced me against a fall, I collected both seat cushions and my makeshift pillow and made my bed on the cockpit deck well. At least now I couldn't fall. I was already on the floor.

I lay there for what seemed like an hour or so without the benefit of sleep. I stood up and did a 360 check—no boats in sight. I couldn't read my watch, so I pressed the business end of a flashlight against the face and energized the radium dial for a few seconds. When I checked it this time, it glowed like it had spent the last couple of days at Chernobyl. It was 2355, almost midnight; I had gotten some sleep after all. I sat groggy, eyes heavy for a couple more minutes. Two minutes later I was lost in some vague thoughts about progress as a sailor.

"Don't you wallow there all pleased with yourself, Buster!"

It was the unmistakable voice of Captain Oakley. He seemed taller than I remembered him, and there was the unmistakable glint of a gold tooth visible even in the near total darkness.

"Sir—"

"You're no sailor yet." A dismissive gesture of his hands cut me off. "When you get serious about this or anything else, you let me know." He leaned forward close enough that I could smell the juniper fragrance of this afternoon's gin on his breath. "Now get up from there and pour me a Captain Morgan."

I dashed below. At the foot of the companionway I turned to see if my visitor was still there. I told myself that I'd gone below to check the time and my position, but if the Captain had still been there I might have poured that Captain Morgan rum.

The GPS said 0136, I must have slept some more or the Captain's visit had been longer than it seemed. I was right on course sailing 324° M at 6.5 knots. Thank heaven for autopilots and steady winds, which were still ENE. I figured they would clock around to east or southeast before dawn. Less than an hour later they were dead southeast at about 10 knots apparent.

The wind shift required some attention. I adjusted the course to 350 to bring the wind a little closer to the beam and trimmed the sails. The apparent wind was hanging around ten knots and we were rolling along at about 5 knots through the water. This was slower, but more importantly much better for sleeping. I didn't know if the winds would go west before morning, but the farther north I went the greater the chances. Just in case I went forward and rigged a preventer (a line fixed to prevent the boom from swinging across the boat in case of a jibe) on the main.

I awoke at 0700 with the sails flogging. The wind had shifted to SW. Good thing I had rigged the preventer. I corrected our alignment to the new winds and reset my course to 310. A few minutes later and *Silk Purse* was making 11 knots over the bottom and about 8 through the sea. I had heard about this type of boost, but had not really believed it.

I checked my position and determined that I was about seventy-five miles east of Titusville, Florida. Perfect. I could ride the Gulf Stream north a while longer. If this held, I would make St. Simons a little sooner than I had planned.

It was almost noon that day when I saw him. He appeared first as a tiny spec in the sky then materialized as a small bird about fifty feet off my transom. His little wings churned the air like a blender whipping up a daiquiri. A moment later he perched on my stern rail, hopped to the helmsman seat, then snuggled in between the combing and the cockpit seat. He was a scruffy brown bird with the general shape of an oversized canary. When I approached a little closer, he puffed out his yellow chest and lifted his wings slightly to make himself more imposing. Inflated now to slightly more than half the size of my fist, he made it clear that he was not a bird with whom I should care to trifle. Making a tactical retreat, I went below to fetch him a drink of water.

I did not know if my visitor was male or female. I describe him here as male since I gave him the name of Carter Canary, after my fellow Georgian and former president. He seemed well-intentioned much in the manner of his namesake. Carter refused my offer of refreshment as he later rebuffed the breadcrumbs, lettuce bits and the last flakes of my Spanish mackerel.

My visitor must have been blown off one of the coastal islands west of me and was simply too exhausted to eat. I sat down across from him trying not to look too rejected. Almost immediately Carter flew/hopped across the cockpit and nested down inside a foot from me. A warm glow of pride passed over me for my St. Francis of Assisi manner with animals. A moment later it became apparent he was using me as a windshield.

A freighter crossed my bow and I went below to try and raise it on the radio. Maybe I could get a weather report. Repeated attempts raised no response and I wondered if anyone was awake.

Carter followed me down the companionway a moment later. I really didn't want him below, but what the heck. A few minutes later Carter was in repose on my bunk. OK, make yourself at home. I wouldn't sleep there before tomorrow night anyway.

Log Entry: 1600 Carter crapped on my bunk and split for parts unknown.

I cleaned up the bird poop and looked everywhere for my guest. He had left without a thank you, a bite me, nothing. Alone again.

From there I continued toward St. Simons Island. As the night wore on, I lost all wind and motored in a dead calm across a polished obsidian sea. The engine droned and we maintained a steady 6.5 knots. I don't know if it was fear of hitting another boat or if I was anxious to get home, but sleep eluded me most of the night.

Finally at 0455 I saw a red light blink on then off. I counted 1, 2, 3, blink, then 1, 2, 3, blink again. It was in the right spot and blinking red every four seconds. This was the STS seabuoy that marked the entrance to the Brunswick Channel. I was home right at forty-seven hours after my departure.

We motored in between the green and red lights until there was light enough in the predawn sky that I recognized the Georgia coast. The Yanmar spun the prop at around 2800 RPM, but we still made slow progress against the obviously ebbing tide. I would prefer to enter my slip on a flood tide since this would place the current on our nose and make securing the boat much easier. I went below and picked up the VHF microphone.

Sid Oakley

"Golden Isles Marina, Golden Isles Marina, *Silk Purse*." I released the transmit button.

"Welcome home, Sid. Let's go to 6–8." I recognized the voice of Clay Parks over the radio. "Where are you? Over."

"I'm still an hour out against this current. Over."

"I've got somebody in your slip, can you tie up on the face dock?"

"Not a problem, Clay. Likely would have anyway with this current. Over."

"Roger that. Golden Isles Marina standing by 1–6."

When I arrived at the docks, I tossed Clay my spring line, then my bowline.

"You by yourself, Sid?" He looked around for any crew on board.

"Yep."

"Wow."

I can't tell you how much I enjoyed hearing that.

The boat in my slip was a Shannon 38, ketch rigged just like Doug's. It had tan canvas, just like Doug's.

"Oh, hell!" I said out loud. "How did he get in here ahead of me?"

I ran across the dock and checked the stern. It read *Comanche* not *Whisper*. You'll never know how relieved I was that Doug had not somehow managed to pass me at sea without my knowledge. It would have been just like him to then put his boat in my slip and quietly wait for me. Just the same, as I headed back to my awaiting bunk, I checked my foredeck for a bag of trash.

A half hour later I pulled the sheet back on my bunk, and there lay Carter Canary dead as a stone. Overcome from exhaustion was my diagnosis.

LESSON: You can overcome your fear, if you just do it.

Chapter 12: *Oh Savannah!*

After I returned from the Abacos, I noticed that the entire state of Georgia was suffering from a group anxiety attack over the impending Olympics. Rumors ran wild. There would be no hotel rooms anywhere near Atlanta. Hotels were to be sold out from Chattanooga, Tennessee all the way to Jacksonville, Florida. There would be a shortage of groceries, over the counter drugs, gasoline, and your favorite wine. I wondered at the time how they knew what my favorite wine might be. Of course, there would be no rental cars available. You could forget buying tickets for an Olympic event, or getting a table in an Atlanta restaurant. And driving in Atlanta, don't even bother to try. Everyone on St. Simons Island was prepared for the biggest influx of tourists ever. There would likely be more people here than in the last five years combined was the general scuttlebutt on the island.

It even became fashionable to bad-mouth the Olympics months before they gave us cause. I remember sitting in one of the mostly locals-only watering holes where most any night shrimpers, bankers, watermen, and real estate brokers gathered to unwind.

"You gonna go up there to them Olympics?" One shrimper asked a Skoal-brother.

"Lemme tell you something, bud." He tongued his tobacco back to the rear of his cheek. "I ain't lost nothing in them Olympics or that Atlanter neither. You?"

"Hell, no. She was wanting to go, but I figured we could wait and go to the Georgie-Florida game. They're gone whoop 'em this year."

Not me, I was going to the Olympics. I couldn't wait for one event.

About an hour in a fast car north of my boat slip the event I was interested in was scheduled. You guessed it, the sailing. My buddy Trey (In earlier versions of this story I changed his name to Ted to spare him undue embarrassment) had moved his boat from Florida to St. Simons and we were soon plotting to sail up to Savannah and take in the sailing. The problem was we called all the local marinas and found that the prices had more than quadrupled to where it would cost upwards of $200 (American!) a night to berth *Silk Purse* at any of the local marinas. Understand please that sailors don't pay $200 to tie up to some dock in Savannah, Georgia. That's a yachtsman thing. There's going to be kings with their vessels tied up here, I was told. Maybe even Jimmy Buffet. That's definite yachtsman territory.

The strange thing was ten days before the Olympics the store shelves were full, St. Simons was empty, and it was a speed limit drive through the streets in Atlanta, something I haven't seen before or since. The hype had scared Georgia residents off to Dollywood, Disney World, or worse. God help them.

A week before we wanted to go, I made a phone call to the Palmer Johnson Marina near the sailing venue in Savannah, and we were able to secure a slip for the Yachting Event for about $40.00 a night. The trip was on. Viva la commoner (the French weren't so out when I first wrote this)! Liberty, Equality, Fraternity!

We left on a Thursday morning with a forecast promising SW winds and perfect summer days. We would take both boats. Trey and his friend David would sail his boat, while Doug and I would bring *Silk Purse*. We left before dawn and motored through the channel against a stiff current until we were able to turn north for Savannah. All the night before, the four of us had insisted that this was to be a relaxed cruise. No racing!

We had a dead south wind of about 12 knots apparent. While I was certain Trey wasn't looking, I snuck my cruising spinnaker along the rail with my cabin top and heel angle acting to hopefully screen my intent. No racing? A ridiculous notion. Anytime two sailboats are heading in the same direction there is always a race.

Tres Bien had about two feet of waterline on us. Still, Doug and I figured that with our hard work and superior abilities it might be close, but we would definitely win. We got smoked.

Our trouble was my cruising chute (spinnaker), depending on your view of life, was either stuck half-open or half-closed. Either way it was definitely half-assed. Trey did a horizon job (to get passed by your competitor so that his boat, mast and all disappears over the horizon) on us. Then he hove-to and waited for us to catch him. Any humility. that I had begun to lose, returned in an instant when I saw him, an hour after he had dropped from sight, waiting for me nose into the wind. I also learned to appreciate my cruising spinnaker for what it truly was—a curse from God.

I turned on the VHF. "All right, let's hear it." He wasn't going to say I couldn't take it.

The radio crackled and the voice of Bobby McFerrin came from the speaker. "Oooo Ooo Oooooo, Don't worry, be happy." A little more static and Trey's voice came across, while Bobby crooned in the background. "We're grilling a few burgers. David opened a bottle of wine. Come on and join us. Better hurry up these things'll spoil at the rate you guys are going."

I could hear the guffaws; I could imagine the knee slapping and high-fives. I was certain then that if there were a God he would help me get back at those guys.

Trey sailed back to meet me with his spinnaker down powered by only his working sails. I was able to keep up easy enough in our no spinnaker class.

Lesson: If you try to employ treachery as a tactic, be certain whom you're fooling.

We continued toward Savannah, and as the afternoon wore on, we saw a line of thunderheads developing along what must have been the shoreline. Trey could track their movement on his radar.

I was too cheap to buy radar and had to depend on his updates. That shouldn't surprise you, since I was also too cheap to buy an anchor windlass. For over a year I had been retrieving my 44 pounds of Bruce anchor, sixty pounds of chain and how much nylon rode I had paid out by the hand-over-hand method. Sometimes this was difficult, while other times it was hard as hell. The cure for this was an expenditure of $1,500.

This might not seem a lot of money when viewed in light of the two hundred thousand dollars I had already invested in *Silk Purse*. But by now my bank balance was reflecting the difficulties my business had been experiencing since the day I took delivery of my new love back at Masonboro Boatyard.

I had also made other decisions based on reducing my negative cash flow such as giving up my apartment in Atlanta. *Silk Purse* and I were now a fulltime item. While I enjoyed this arrangement, it did nothing to address my business or personal problems—just the opposite. The fact was, for some reason, I didn't care. I had always managed to work things out in the past, and now I managed to convince myself things would work out again. Just not right now.

This is not as unrelated a tangent as it might at first seem. Wherever I sailed on *Silk Purse,* I was unable to completely elude my problems. I thought of them as being back in Atlanta, but if that was true how could they unerringly find me thirty miles offshore? Maybe I hadn't gone far enough. Self-deception, it can be sweet.

The radio buzzed to life. "*Silk Purse, Tres Bien* on 71."

As a matter of practice, boats in our group monitored channel 71. This meant that we would avoid the chatter on 16, the hailing channel, and also avoid the necessity of constantly switching to a working frequency.

"Yeah, Trey." Doug answered.

"This squall line is heading our way. We're certain to get hit by one of the cells. Over."

"Better reef that main while you can." Doug advised.

Trey's radio was silent for a moment. "My main is a lot smaller than Sid's. I'm not concerned about it."

"You're the Captain."

The sail configuration on Trey's boat was different from mine. He had more of the sail area in his headsail combination and thus a smaller main than I did. So technically he was correct.

When Doug returned topside, I was already tying down the reef in our main sail.

"I'll roll in the stays'l," Doug said. "That shouldn't affect our speed too much."

"Less than half a knot." I looked at the dark clouds that were bearing down on us and pointed toward them. "We'll have company soon."

We continued on course under single-reefed main and full genoa with our speed bouncing around 6 knots. Trey, still fully powered, passed us again. But this time I didn't mind so much. That thought had barely formed when it hit us.

In an instant the winds veered and jumped from 15 apparent to over 30. We brought *Silk Purse* around in time to avoid an accidental jibe, and she heeled hard to starboard.

"Let's get that jib in!" Doug pointed at the headsail.

I grabbed the furling line and Doug released some tension from the sheet. I pulled the line hard against the ratchet block, but I could make no headway against the wind that had built well past the thirty knots we'd seen a moment ago.

"Clear the winch." I tried to point and hold the furling line at the same time.

Doug had it free of the jib sheet before the words were out of my mouth. I strained against the furling line not wanting to lose even an inch as I wrapped it clockwise around the primary winch. Doug gave me the winch handle, and a second later I was cranking the jib in. By the time I got half of the headsail furled we were pretty much upright, but I cranked her in until I noticed the rat's nest of line kicking around the port bow. The lazy sheet (line not currently employed in controlling a sail) had managed to tie itself in a huge knot. Before I could react the lazy sheet jumped across the bow and immediately entangled my working sheet so that I was unable to completely furl the jib (genoa, terms are incorrectly but often used interchangeably). If left untended, the sheets would flog around until they damaged the genoa. By now, the wind was gusting well past 50 knots, and the cluster of lines grew bigger every second.

I hooked my tether to one of the jacklines that was rigged the length of the boat and worked my way forward. When I got where I could reach the gnarled lines, I hooked myself both port and starboard so that I could focus my attention on straightening the sheets. The mess proved to look worse than it actually was, and inside five minutes I was back in the cockpit.

By the time I got back, Doug had the jib secured.

"Sid! Look at that!" Doug pointed across the water toward *Tres Bien*.

I looked just in time to see the boom recoil from what must have been one serious accidental jibe. When a sailboat turns its stern through the wind, the maneuver is called a jibe. If this is done in a controlled manner, it is a safe and efficient method to change tacks. An uncontrolled jibe can be extremely dangerous since the main boom can swing in a viscous arc across the deck of the boat causing injury to anyone or anything in its path.

That's what I did see. What I didn't see was Trey or David.

"Where the hell are they?" I screamed at Doug like it was his fault.

"I don't know!" Doug yelled back at me, as he hopped down the companionway.

"*Tres Bien, Tres Bien, Tres Bien!*"

I heard Doug on the radio and swung our bow in the direction of our friends just in time to see their boom slam back across the boat in another jibe. What was going on?

"*Tres Bien, Tres Bien.* Trey, answer the radio!"

A few seconds later we got an answer: "Doug, we've lost our steering…can't talk."

"Trey secure that boom or you're gonna lose your rig."

Doug was right. They wouldn't be the first to lose their mast to an uncontrolled jibe. No sooner had that thought entered my mind than the boom swung over again, though not as violently this time. Next I saw Trey emerge from below and sheet his main down tight. That secured the boat against immediate danger.

"I've lost steering and there is no emergency tiller onboard." Trey's voice came back over the VHF. "I swear I saw one when I was looking to buy this boat."

"I remember seeing one too when Sid and I looked at it with you. Over." Doug said. A degree of calm was settling back over our group.

"Yeah," I said. "It was under the aft cabin bunk."

"Hey guys," Trey came back. "You two saw the first boat I looked at, not the one I bought."

He was right Doug and I saw that first Offshore 40 he looked at, but it was sold before Trey could make an offer. He had found this sister ship and bought it more or less on the spot.

Did this mean I would have to tow in the guy who had just done a horizon job on me? Could I be that lucky? That would sure shut up all that horizon job talk. Oh God, if you're really up there, please let that happen. Let me tow him in, and I won't ask for anything else 'til Christmas.

"I think I can steer us into port using the autopilot. It still works."

Oh well, I suppose some things are too good to be true.

Trey found that if he doused his sails and used the course change buttons on the autopilot, he could actually steer fairly well. This was possible because the autopilot is connected directly to the rudderpost and works independent of the cable steering mechanism. There were two sets of buttons on his autopilot: a ten-degree port and starboard pair, and a one-degree port and starboard pair. If he pushed the ten-degree starboard button once, the boat slowly turned ten degrees right. Punch it twice and the boat turned twenty degrees right. Two ten-degree adjustments right followed by three one-degree left adjustments and he would net out an approximately seventeen degrees right course adjustment. It took some time and lacked any degree of finesse, but it should get him to the docks at least. Getting the boat docked with the autopilot would take some doing.

The plan called for us to sail ahead, and Trey to follow in our wake. We could radio him any necessary course adjustments required. We sailed past the sea buoy marking Wassaw Sound Channel then turned to a course of 309° M to enter the marked channel. That's when the security boardings began.

We were visited by the Coast Guard, the Department of Natural Resources (DNR), the Coast Guard again, and finally U.S. Customs. The customs officials approached us on a sleek Fountain thirty-five footer that could out run the word of the Lord. Yeah, these guys were pulling tough duty. Of the bunch the only group that seemed to know what they were doing was the DNR.

Coast Guard: "Where are you coming from?"

Sailor: "St. Simons Island."

Coast Guard: "Where's that? "

Sailor: "You're not from around here, are you?"

Customs: "Have you guys been to the Bahamas?"

Sailor: "Yeah, got back a couple of months ago. How about y'all?"

Customs: "You guys are not coming from the Bahamas now, are you?"

Sailor: "Like we told all the others, we're coming from St. Simons Island."

Customs: "That's not in the Bahamas is it?"

Sailor: "Isn't anyone from around here?"

Customs: "You boys got any drugs or contraband?"

Sailor: "No sir. Just Budweiser."

I was disappointed that he didn't want to know if Budweiser was in the Bahamas, but I didn't want to wise off too much because there were still two Kalick beers on board that I had forgotten to drink on the way back from the Bahamas. I had figured that I would drink them about ten miles off shore because I didn't think there was an import duty on urine.

We continued through the inlet and into the ICW. Just before 10 p.m.we saw the lights of the Palmer Johnson Marina. There wasn't another boat on the entire dock. Doug and I tied up and stood ready to catch Trey's lines. He did a masterful job of docking that boat with only the autopilot for steering.

OK, now I have a question for you. Who won the race?

The next morning the waterway was filled with weekend warriors buzzing around in their red inflatables. The Coast Guard and DNR were out in full force as well. This was probably what the Bay of Pigs invasion force looked like. It didn't take us long to learn that we would not be allowed to anchor out and watch the races that day or any other. We would have to take a party boat and watch. This sounded like peeking through a bunch of other people's heads, while their kids screamed and ran all over the boat. No thank you.

Maybe there was a bar or pavilion with closed circuit TV. Nope. Who was in charge of marketing this event? Probably, those Customs guys we met yesterday.

That morning we repaired the steering on *Tres Bien*. It was a bit of a makeshift job, but everyone felt certain it would serve until we could get back to St. Simons. We spent the day looking for T-shirts and the evening in debauchery. Late that night Trey awoke to find that NBC had a live news report on the tube. He checked his watch to find that it was not yet 4 a.m.. This must be important. It was. Some jackass had set off a bomb in Olympic Park.

We awoke the next morning to find that yesterday's security armada was now armed with machine guns mounted in the bows of their inflatables. (I swear!) In addition to the side arms they carried the day before, these guys were now each holding some sort of Uzi type gun. All I could think of was Larry, Curly, and the boys meet automatic weapons. It wasn't hard to persuade our troop to retreat on down the waterway.

We motored generally south up the Wilmington River. About 5 miles later we followed the ICW into the Skiddaway River. As we left the Wilmington River, the noise and confusion generated by the misfortune in Atlanta fell away. For the next hour the only boat we met was a small skiff handled by a waterman checking his crab traps. The dark water coiled its way through the muted hues of green and golden grasses. Herons and cormorants lifted their heads toward the sun, while pelicans roosted with a lazy grace. We approached Grimball Point, and Doug silently pointed across the marsh to our right. A lone pine skeleton stood sentinel over the marsh. In its crest hovering over a nest of driftwood and grass, an Osprey dropped a small fish to a pair of hungry beaks.

"It won't be long before those two are on their own," Doug said.

"Yeah," I felt a gentle warmth spreading in my chest, "wonder if they'll ever realize how good they have it now?"

Doug went below and soon emerged with two Miller Lites. "I'll drive awhile," he said, handing me a beer.

"There are some advantages to being an adult."

I gave up the helm to my brother and took advantage of his current good nature. Normally, he will only steer a boat in the waterway if directly threatened with a weapon or bribed with an adult beverage. We had a total of about a hundred statute miles to motor before reaching Golden Isles Marina. This would take the better part of two days and I did not like steering much better than Doug did.

We rounded a gentle bend in the river. Ahead, nestled behind an elbow of water was Isle of Hope. Stately low country homes looked out across the Skiddaway River with a lack of pretension that can only be acquired after decades of esteem. A copse of ancient live oaks laced with Spanish moss kept silent watch over this genteel southern community. I couldn't help but wonder what stories and secrets these old patriarchs harbored, but would never tell.

I reached across Doug and pushed the throttle into idle.

"Let's not hurry through here," I said.

"I was thinking the same thing."

We continued past the small anchorage until the river narrowed to a ribbon of tea colored water. I pointed a finger ahead of us to make certain Doug had seen the small bascule bridge. He nodded in recognition, and I realized that neither of us had spoken since passing Isle of Hope. Doug stood up and went below. I took the helm and put the Yanmar in neutral. A gentle current pushed us toward the bridge, and when we got within fifty yards I pulled us into reverse. We would wait here for Trey. There was no sense in making the bridge tender open twice.

I heard the radio scratch to life and a moment later the bridge tender called us. "Cap, y'all want an opening here this morning?"

"There's another boat behind us," Doug answered. "Might as well wait on him."

"I 'preciate that."

Once through the bridge the Skiddaway empties into the Moon River. It wasn't wider than a mile, but it's not hard to understand why someone might pen a song about it. We motored on south and crossed the Little Ogeechee then the Ogeechee Rivers. The local population refers to these as the Lil' Geech and the Geech and if you ask about either of the Ogeechees by their proper name you will most likely be met with a blank stare or a disgusted shake of the head.

We continued through what is generally known as the Florida Passage, past Kilkenny Creek, down the Bear River, and finally we crossed St. Catherines Sound. It was late afternoon, almost evening and both of us had tired of steering. We had motored a long way with little liquid sustenance, and we felt anxious to amend our deprived condition. It was time to anchor.

We checked the chart looking for a spot that would be out of the way of any boat traffic and out of the open fetch of St Catherines Sound. About a mile south of the North Newport River we saw a likely spot. We had time to check it out before Trey caught up. (His boat might sail a little faster than mine, but it motored much more slowly.) The ICW bent east of a perfect sized finger of water that snuggled against the western shore. A sand bar rose from the bottom to offer protection from any boat wakes formed on the ICW. It looked as near perfect as we were apt to find without going well out of our way.

We entered the anchorage slightly north of ICW day marker 122. I circled through the area and decided it would do nicely for a number of boats to have lots of room to swing on their hooks. Taking no chances with the shifting tidal currents, I buried my 44-pound Bruce anchor and most of my fifty feet of chain in the black Georgia mud, then let out enough nylon rode to give me an 8:1 scope when high tide arrived. We would swing a bit, but we could rest easy until morning.

Doug and I each took a shower in the cockpit. The day had been a hot one and my skin was salt encrusted, much like those six dollar baked potatoes you get at the fancy steak houses. The cool fresh water felt good, and there was enough of a breeze that the mosquitoes were not a problem. About the time we got air-dried and comfortable, Trey arrived in the anchorage.

His idea was that we raft up and share resources for dinner. Although I had never had a mishap rafting two boats together, this is not a practice I like for any length of time.

But Trey's idea to share dinner sounded good because the day before I saw several filets on his boat and we had beans and weenies on my boat. I set out my largest fenders and caught Trey's lines as he slowly came alongside. We tied the boats together bow and stern and set a tight spring line fore and aft. We would hang on my anchor until after dinner then push off *Tres Bien*. They would spend the night on their own anchor.

The filets were wonderful, and I made a black bean and orzo salad to go with them. Believe it or not, I had a loaf of sourdough bread. Add that to a good cabernet, and you've got quite a feast. The next thing I know David produced a bottle of port and we retired topside for our after dinner toasts.

Needless to say, none of us was in any shape to push Trey's boat off and get him safely anchored. We figured there was less chance of a screw up spending the night tied together than trying to anchor under the influence.

Sometime in the middle of the night I heard, or rather felt, the hull shutter like someone had snapped a huge rubber band against its side right near my head. I got up, went topside, and looked around, but everything looked OK. Thirty seconds later I was again collapsed in my bunk.

The next morning I got up. It wasn't particularly early. I made a cup of coffee and crawled topside hoping against logic that it would kick the cobwebs from my head. David was up and seemed a bit puzzled. I allowed him his thoughts without any input from me.

A couple of minutes later Trey sounded across the water like a bull moose in heat. "Where the hell are we?" He sprung out the companionway of his boat and two steps later he was at the bow. "We've drug a mile—two miles from where we were last night."

"Bull," I said, ever the clever one in the morning. I climbed out to the bow. "You're right." We definitely were not in the anchorage where we turned in. "I can't believe we drug that far on that anchor."

"Oh God," Doug said as he crawled out from below. "He's right, Sid. This is not where I went to sleep. I'm turning on the GPS, at least it won't be lost."

I ran back to the cockpit and checked the compass. Due east of us there was a sea of marsh grass that stretched well past where I remembered leaving the ocean last night. Where the Davey Jones were we? I still couldn't believe that anchor had failed like that. I mean, even if it had broken loose, and I didn't believe that, how could it have failed to reset?

Trey untied his boat from *Silk Purse*.

"I'm going that way." He pointed up current. "If it looks like the way out of here, I'll call you on the radio."

I went to the bow and began to retrieve the anchor with my hand over hand windlass. I pulled up about ten feet of rode with no resistance, which was not uncommon. The next pull or so would bring tension on the line, and my work would begin in earnest. Not this time. The next pull of the line brought a naked end of line into my hand. There was a residue of blue bottom paint on the line.

Suddenly everything became clear. *Tres Bien* had lain with her keel against my anchor rode. The twang we heard in the night was the line parting when Trey's boat had sawed through our rode enough to make it too weak to hold us.

"Look here, Sid," Doug yelled at me. "We're off the ICW chart or this GPS is lost." He saw me staring at the parted rode. "Oh, I guess the GPS knows where we are after all."

I dropped the secondary anchor and let it set itself on short scope. We would stay where we were until we knew where to go. I went below and Doug pointed to a spot on the nav table about six inches off the chart.

"I figure we're about here. You got another chart."

I pulled a chart from my drawer and soon we found where we were, OK. But both of us wanted to retrace what must have been our route the night before because neither of us could believe it.

"This way is wrong," we heard David over the radio. "We're coming back toward y'all."

"We've got our position on a chart," Doug answered. "You won't believe it."

By checking the chart we retraced the only route that would have taken us from where we had been to where we were.

After the line parted with the twang that would have been a clear sign to sober people, we all went back to sleep while more than fifty thousand pounds of tied together sailboats drifted on the incoming tide. We went a mile south on the ICW, then made a sweeping right hand turn through more than a hundred degrees and over a sandbar that is all but dry at low tide. We continued up what the charts call the Timmons River.

I'm talking about twenty-six feet by forty-two feet of tied together boats spinning slowly in the brown waters of coastal Georgia. Close your eyes. I'll bet "seamanship" is not the caption for the picture in your mind.

So our almost 1,100 square foot raft somehow manages to turn west over a sandbar and then twirls its way another mile and a half up the Timmons River where the slumbering occupants find themselves once they regain consciousness.

In route to our present position our barge missed no less than nine docks, at least half of them had boats we could

Raise the Sails

have crushed and later replaced. We skirted several opportunities to run aground. The chance of costly boat damage in a grounding while rafted together increases exponentially, I'm sure. Had the tide been on the ebb we would have been swept out to sea. Talk about a shock when you get up to dribble over the rail. Once out the inlet, the chances of being grounded on a bar, beach, or rock formation are excellent. Either of these would probably result in the loss of both boats, not to mention lives.

So I am fortunate, make that downright lucky, to be out a four hundred-fifty dollar anchor, plus chain, and a hundred feet of nylon rode. Is it any wonder that when Doug and I looked each other in the eye all we saw was embarrassment?...Yep, we're sitting up the Timmons mortified beyond description.

In typical Oakley boy fashion, we renamed the river; it's now a creek. I bet you can guess the name. As we motored the rest of the way to St. Simmons, we made up a song. You can sing it if you want to. It goes to the tune of the Village People's YMCA. We even made up body signals for the crucial letters. I see a future in show biz for the "Oakley Bouyz". Maybe we can get someone younger to do the letters, because my back spasms every time I try to get into the S position.

> *Young girls! Do you want to go sail?*
> *I said young girls, do you want to go cruise?*
> *All you need is a boat and some booze!*
> *And we can sail up the S H _ T! (remember the signs)*
> *I wanna sail up the S H _ T!*
> *It's the only creek that's fit for me.*
> *I said the S H _ T!*
> *Let's sail up the S H _ T!*

That's the song, and that's the story. However, I do have one request. If you are a sailor or decide to become one, and if you are ever in the ICW between Savannah and St. Simons, stop by marker 122 and pick up my anchor. We went back twice and tried to find it, but that's another story.

Lessons: Too numerous to name. When I replaced my anchor, I bought another Bruce. However, this time I bought 200 feet of 3/8 chain. Saw through that!

Chapter 13: *At Last*

I meant to leave on my fiftieth birthday. I didn't make it, but only missed by a few weeks.

By early March I was finally ready. I was going cruising. It wouldn't be the circumnavigation or even the three-year Caribbean escape of my dreams. But I was going for a while with no set timetable. As I sat on *Silk Purse's* bow pulpit watching the last crimson rays of light retreating over the salt marsh, I wondered when I would return to Golden Isles Marina and St. Simons Island. My plans were to sail south from the island, first to the Florida Keys then to the Bahamas Cays (remember it's pronounced keys no matter what those fishing shows on TV say). The trip might be extended down to the Dominican Republic, and Venezuela wasn't out of the question, especially if I stayed out well into hurricane season. Somewhere in the foggier recesses of my mind the concept began to form that it was unimportant where I went, but it was most important that I go.

I had made a bit of a life for myself on St. Simons, but I couldn't earn a living. It wasn't just the trust-fund-baby environment of the island; it also was living on a sailboat that contributed to my being unproductive. These were two influences I might have overcome if I had been of sound mental health. I realized as darkness settled over me that the following day would mark one solid year since I had made a deposit into a personal bank account. Two years ago the thought that I would allow an anniversary like that to occur would never have entered my mind. Tonight, like so many nights in the past year, I was unable to force myself to care.

In the morning, I promised myself to place sensibility on hold (as if that were anything new) for an unspecified time and go sailing. For the first time, I would leave without a schedule. I knew a few places I would go, after that my mind was open. A seed of hope for Judi and me that hadn't been there a few weeks ago had just begun to sprout. That was definitely a place I planned to visit, maybe stay.

I said my good-byes that night to all my island friends. A party broke out at the Dockside Bar, and on that night at least, my money was no good. Despite several rounds of brews and chardonnay that I had yet to collect, I slipped back to the boat. I turned on the TV and found a rerun of the old Horatio Hornblower movie that I watched for the twentieth time until dropping off to sleep on the settee in the salon.

The next morning I was up well before dawn. The marine forecast on NOAA radio was not favorable to sailing south offshore. It would be down the ditch this morning. Offshore would come soon enough.

At 0645 I backed out of the slip that had been home to me for a little over a year, and to *Silk Purse* for two. I was off cruising, first the Keys then the Bahamas. By 0715 the autopilot went out. All day long it would work a minute or two or an hour or so then crap out. Not being able to trust it was as bad as it not steering. Where is your little brother when you need him? I have plenty of adult beverages so he could be persuaded to steer.

After crossing St. Simons Sound, *Silk Purse* found her way through the entrance to the ICW, and we motored down the ditch between Jekyll Island and the mainland. The waterway here is a thread of dark water coiling its way through a sea of grass until it empties into the St Andrews Sound. When the wind blows along the water the grass undulates as if as an unseen, giant serpent were swimming through the marsh.

Once in the sound a west wind built, and I raised the main and set the jib. I killed the diesel, and when the silence replaced the rumble of the engine things changed. Instead of watching the marsh go by, as would be the case in an automobile or even a powerboat, we became part of the seascape. Same place, same boat, same driver: the only thing that had changed was perception.

Could it be that perception can sometimes be more important than the truth? My answer in a few months time would be quite different from the one I would have offered on that day.

Regardless of our philosophy, it remains true that under power, even a sailboat is simply passing through the marsh.

Raise the Sails

Raise the sails and the arrival of silence is not the only change; now the motion of the boat becomes harmonious with the sea. Under sail, *Silk Purse* and her passenger become part of the environment. If you were a painter alone on the beach and standing in front of your easel, you would have brushed *Silk Purse* on your canvass as naturally as if she were the grass or the sea.

As if to confirm this, a pod of small spotted dolphin raced toward the boat. A moment later what might have been as many as a half dozen dark gray, spotted bodies displayed perfect group harmony by taking turns riding my bow wave without the assistance of proper parliamentary procedure.

Harmony, perhaps I would find it.

I was able to sail across St. Andrews Sound and down the northwest shore of Cumberland Island, where the waterway is more like a lake than a creek. By now, the sun was nearly as high as my mood, and across the water I saw a small herd of the scruffy ponies that run wild on Cumberland Island. Good omens abound. When the waterway narrowed and the wind became squirrelly, I had to roll up the jib and crank the diesel. Once again, we became mere spectators to the beauty around us.

I motored to Fernandina and dropped the hook within fifty feet of where memory told me the trawler had moored to a crab pot marker. I opened the boat to let as much air in as possible and began to dissect the autopilot. An hour later I had it fixed in a makeshift fashion. The housing for the fuse that protected its circuit had gotten itself cracked and a bit of electrical tape got us in working order. I would replace the housing before leaving the States.

The next morning I delayed our departure so that I could pass through Nassau Sound an hour or so before high tide. The route through there is notorious for grounding sailboats, and I didn't want to be a victim of those shifting shallows. With nearly six feet of extra water over the bottom at high tide, there would be little chance of my running hard aground.

Over the next week or so I made my way past the Ponce de Leon inlet. I spent three days in St. Augustine and two visiting Harold, a friend in Daytona.

Silk Purse and I left Daytona on an early ebb tide backtracking toward open ocean. Midmorning I spun the wheel to my right and *Silk Purse* swung her nose eastward and through the Ponce de Leon inlet. As the jetties dropped out of sight over our stern, I took my first wave over the bow. That splash of brine seemed to wash away any lingering melancholy. I had a seaway under my keel for the first time this trip. The adventure I had been making ready to begin for two years crystallized in my brain as the east wind tossed another bucket of seawater across my bow. By God, I was really on my way! I was a sailor at last, and more than that, I had an appointment waiting just south of Ft. Pierce with what might well be my future re-found.

Chapter 14: *Coastal Cruising*

I cleared the Ponce de Leon inlet and set a course that would take me between the shoals that lie off Cape Canaveral. According to the NOAA weather report, the winds were blowing SSW, but unless the compass and the GPS were engaged in some sort of conspiracy the wind was blowing from the east at 12–15 knots. This meant good conditions for a course of 155° M, which is what I needed to make my first waypoint. This was a somewhat arbitrary point that I had picked that placed me between the Chester shoal to my west and the Hetzel Shoal east. If I missed the waypoint and ran over either shoal, the water was not shallow enough to be dangerous. Of course, if there happened to be an uncharted obstruction lurking in ten feet of water that would constitute a hazard. Once past Chester Shoal, I would turn almost due south. I was convinced that there I would meet those SSW winds NOAA was predicting. It is a well-known fact among sailors that once a course receives a firm commitment, Neptune and all his minions will stop at nothing to get the wind on your nose.

I negotiated the some thirty miles to my first waypoint in a little less than five hours. The B&G speed/log (knot meter, measures speed through the water) had shown an average of a little over 7 knots for the trip, but the GPS (speed over the bottom) had consistently read a knot and a half slower. This meant that I was experiencing a head current of a knot or more. Neptune was smiling.

Currents can set a vessel to either side or on the nose. On those wonderful occasions when it is on your stern, you can get a significant lift like I experienced returning from the Abacos the year before. I can also remember a time sailing into St. Simons Sound against a current so strong that my knot meter claimed that we were moving along at something less than 7 knots, while it required several minutes to go the forty feet required to pass a green channel marker. It wasn't until I fired up the Yanmar that *Silk Purse* was able to make significant headway against the exiting tide.

I'm off on this tangent for a purpose. This situation is a clear example of the difference between knot meter readings and speed over the bottom. The knot meter was, of course, measuring the speed of water passing over its sensor, which was mostly the current. The green can indicated my speed over the bottom, which was essentially zero.

About two hours later I passed the next waypoint and turned south. I estimate that it took about thirty minutes to find those south winds. NOAA was finally right. I could no longer carry the jib, and the staysail was useless. I furled both of these and pulled the main into the centerline of the boat. NOAA was also predicting a cold front to reach the area sometime before morning. This would bring northwesterly winds that would be most welcome, until then I would be compelled to endure the *put-put-put* of the Yanmar. Neptune and crew were dancing a jig.

I started to feel my eyelids getting heavy, but sleep was a bad idea this close to shore and shoals. Another reason to stay awake was that ahead I could barely make out random lights scattered around like ducks on a pond. I decided this was an armada of local fishermen out in boats not much larger than my dink. Since I didn't have a shotgun, the only way to harvest this flock would be to mow them down with the bow of the boat. For that I would be required to stay awake. Just kidding!

I was certain I could get a couple even if I went to sleep. However, this was certain to cause a huge delay in my cruise, while I dug my way from under the mountain of paper such an incident would create.

Fortunately, I was prepared for just such an occasion. I went below and a minute later emerged with my (I swear) 1,000,000 candlepower spotlight. It had a long coiled cord that allowed me to take it all the way to the bow. You might remember the autopilot had a portable controller with similarly long cord. I went forward electric beam and tiller in tow and feeling a little like a deathstar captain on a search and destroy mission. Only these guys bobbing on the wavelets in their little boats were sure to be grateful that I had taken such extraordinary precautions in favor of their safety. I mean I could run my thirty plus thousand pounds of boat and stowage over one of these guys and hardly know I'd hit him.

The first boat began to take shape less than a hundred yards off my port bow. I would likely miss them with no course change, but better safe than sorry. When they were about a hundred feet away, I picked up the searchlight, aimed it, and thumbed that baby on. It hummed to life, and squirmed in my hand like a boa constrictor.

The little boat ahead of me was set ablaze in the blue-white flame of 1,000,000 candlepower. There were two men in the boat and half a dozen fishing rigs set up three to each side. The fisherman in the stern jerked his face around shielding his eyes from my deathstar ray. The man in the bow simply covered his eyes with one hand and held his other hand up in a well-known international salute.

I made a quick course adjustment, doused my ray gun and stumbled, half-blinded myself, back to the cockpit. I tossed the light below with the firm resolution not to use it again unless boarded by pirates.

I looked forward and there was a second boat, this time off my starboard bow. After the experience with the light I decided to maneuver unassisted by candlepower. I turned about fifteen degrees to port that should have left him well to my right, but a minute later he stilled bobbed in the water in the same relative position. I gave her another fifteen-degree turn to port and sure enough he was still there. The other boats seemed to be standing still while this poor devil had been elected scapegoat. Maybe they thought that if I chased after him the rest were sure to escape. Now my fisherman was dead ahead. This told me that my tactics were not effective, so I spun the wheel to starboard and missed the two guys by about twenty feet. Way too close! It must have been good for fishing though because, just as my stern passed by them, two of the rods on their port side bent like crazy as the line spooled off their reels.

I returned to the bow to get an unassisted view of the next boat ahead. The guys I had just maneuvered around must have been really pulling in a catch because I could still hear the occasional expletive bouncing across the water.

My new tactic would be to watch from this improved vantage point for the next bobbing light and maybe such a close call could be avoided. This wasn't the problem that it had been earlier. Ahead of me there were noticeably fewer lights than there had been ten minutes earlier. As I motored along in the quiet evening, I became aware of a definite parting of the lights ahead of me. I went to the cockpit to get a compass check and observed that the lights were actually filling in behind me as my wake passed. I returned to my watch station only to see the little lights migrating either to port or starboard. I wondered if this was how Moses felt when he saw the Red Sea part in front of him then come back together in his wake. Well, maybe not.

An hour past the fishing boats, the cold front caught up with us, and we had a modest wind that blew first from the west then from the northwest. I doused the Yanmar and rolled out the jib. Quiet descended over my little world and *Silk Purse* and I cruised south on a most hypnotic broad reach.

We continued south and as the Florida coast fell away to the west, I was able to relax, though I still felt it imperative to remain awake. I stretched out in the cockpit to get some rest. Every ten minutes I stood erect and completed a 360° check—no boats, no visible lights: good news. A few minutes before 0200 I jerked awake from a dead sleep. Without realizing it, I had pulled a throwable cushion under my head for a pillow and curled into a fetal ball for a few Z's. A quick circumspect revealed that luck was with me; there were no impending disasters. Coffee! I went below, put on a pot of water to boil and checked the GPS for position. Everything was perfect, and in a few minutes I emerged with a huge thermos of strong and overly sweetened java. Half an hour later a caffeine buzz had replaced my case of the nods.

I remember thinking that *Silk Purse* must be a lucky vessel to avoid disaster, especially when she had a donkey for a captain.

Log Entry: 0530 Ft. Pierce inlet bearing 176° M, range 6 miles. S 6.7, C 174° M Should be through inlet by dawn 0630

My log entry proved accurate and I dropped the main once inside the jetties. We motored south down the ICW to Jensen Beach. At 1015 I dropped the hook in about ten feet of water. When *Silk Purse* swung her nose into the 12 knot NW wind, I went below and popped open the hatches. They would catch the breeze and make for comfortable conditions below.

At the nav station, I checked my instruments; the log for this leg read 171 miles. Total for the trip was 322 miles. I had done over half the total trip since leaving Halifax Marina in Daytona a little over 24 hours ago. I went forward, took a nice shower, and then fell naked into the bunk for a little nap.

Lesson: Coastal sailing as a single hander can be more dangerous than an ocean voyage. If those fishing boats had been freighters, my nap might have been permanent and somewhere off the Florida coast.

Chapter 15: *Hope*

Sunlight forced its way through my shut lids, and I tried to hide my eyes in the crook of an elbow. When that didn't work, I rolled over away from the sun. When that didn't work, I gave in to morning and stretched myself awake. Sometime last night I remembered getting up and coming to the cockpit. I had been restless and in that half-asleep state that can be either restful or fretful depending on your mood. This was my second night in the Jensen Beach anchorage and I was anxious for the new day to begin.

Today was a big day for me. Judi was coming. I was hopeful that she, like me, harbored a renewed hope that our lives could be restarted together. She wasn't due until sometime after noon, but I began cleaning the boat in anticipation. Not that it particularly needed it. *Silk Purse* was generally clean and orderly; it's a matter of seamanship. This practice did not then, nor does it now, extend to other phases of my life. I'm not a dirty person, but clutter seems to follow me around like a puppy. I mean you should see my sock drawer. Pardon the sock drawer tangent, but I am apparently attempting to put

Raise the Sails

off admitting that I was nervous as squirrel in a dog pen about our long weekend together.

I wasn't concerned that Judi and I would not have a good time. That was part of our problem. I had skipped my way through the years in our marriage that most husbands spend making plans, acquiring stuff, and becoming a father. Whistling in the dark, can you pick out the tune? Instead of a son or daughter I had a wine cork collection that would impress Robert Parker, if not for quality then certainly for volume. It took a lot of soul searching and a couple of dollars in therapy for me to realize one thing. Since I had been denied a childhood when I was of the age to have one, I had spent the last twenty-five years experiencing childhood as an adult.

Could that be the reason I have no children? Introspection tells me I am on the right track, if not completely correct.

OK, so now you're comfortable that I'm not fearful about the two of us having a good time. However, when I finished scrubbing the head and the galley was shining like a new dime, I still felt like some sort of anxiety download was on its way. My uneasiness centered on talking. I wasn't afraid of what we might say. I was afraid that we would not talk at all, at least talk of nothing with substance. Would we spend this time together and not address our core issues? We both knew what our core issues were. After all both of us had worked those things out with an effective, loving, and friendly MD, PC.

The problem was my lips were beginning to pucker. That Zippy De Do Da melody was forming and Judi had yet to arrive.

By the time I showered and put on a look-dirty-but-clean pair of shorts, it was almost time for her to show. I went topside. Less than five minutes passed, and she was waving to me from shore. My heart butterflied, and I could feel the grin on my face. She looked good to me in a number of ways.

I hopped in the dink and fetched her back to *Silk Purse*. Both my girls were with me now, and I was content as those cows that used to supply the Carnation folks with all their milk. The two women were as different in personality as in appearance. Judi was tall, thin, and shapely; *Silk Purse* was more long and heavy with a sturdy foot beneath her. Variety is the spice of life.

Our time together passed well. We went biking along the beaches on Hutchinson Island, toured the area looking for that perfect restaurant, and made peace with each other. We also made plans to discuss our future together. Sooner than I thought possible, it was time for her to leave.

Before our life could be resumed, there was still some unfinished business. I was determined to take *Silk Purse* to South America or at least to Georgetown, Bahamas.

It is not that I was ambivalent about Judi and me; I was ambivalent about life.

"Are you going back to Georgia to get that girl, sailor?" It was the harsh voice of Captain Oakley.

This time he was dressed in a more modern day naval uniform. I remember admiring the bright polish of his belt buckle. Easy enough for him to be all spit shined I thought. He is never around long enough to get a salt tarnish on his brass. That might not be all bad either.

"Sir! Yes, sir!" I answered and resisted the urge to snap to attention.

"Then, get those South America thoughts out of your head! South America my backside, have you balanced your checkbook lately, sailor?"

"It's an ugly story, sir."

"You tend your business! South America will still be there a hundred years from now."

Thankfully Captain Oakley evaporated before he gained enough substance to actually grab me by the ear. Thankfully he didn't dress me down until Judi was on her way to the airport. He might be hard to explain.

Chapter 16: *Your Watch*

The morning after Judi departed I headed down the ICW toward Lake Worth (Palm Beach) with a clear sky and a partly cloudy future. I felt pleased that Judi and I might be able to work out our lives, but for the near time, my focus was on this trip. The thought kept harassing me that at a minimum the trip must reach Georgetown, Exuma, Bahamas, or it would an incomplete experience and a failure. I would later learn that no matter the distance sailed, the ports visited, or the people met, the experience must by its very nature remain incomplete. There would always be another horizon, another sheltered harbor where I could drop the hook. What mattered was the experience itself, what was taken from it, and what was left with the people visited.

At the moment my sights were set on leaving something with the people in Key West.

We (*Silk Purse*, me, and perhaps Captain Oakley) continued down the ditch until we passed the St. Lucie inlet. I resisted the urge to exit there because of a still vivid memory of Doug and me running a powerboat aground on one of the inlet's shifting shoals. That boat drew only about two feet of water, and we were able to push it off the shoal with little difficulty. That would not be the case if I grounded *Silk Purse*.

A little farther south we reached Hobe Sound. I took advantage of the long distance visibility to set the autopilot and go below. Right now, before I got tired or stressed out, I would find that Captain Oakley and either come to terms with him or he could walk the plank. Harrr! I was not going to take his bullying this entire trip. I didn't care how good his *advice* was. However, after a couple of minutes searching below, I realized that he was not to be found no matter how thorough my search. He would reveal himself to me, or he would not. Maybe it was some sun block I had come down here to retrieve.

That afternoon we reached the Lake Worth area. After a couple of great nights in the Old Port anchorage just north of the inlet, we left in search of adventure in the Florida Keys. I exited protected waters about 1500 (3 p.m. lubber time) planning to sail south past Ft. Lauderdale, Miami, and Key Largo. The timing was not an accident. Rather it reflected my wish to not enter Hawk Channel and the water around the Keys at night. This departure time would mean our arrival there should coincide with sunrise.

I turned south under full main, genoa, and staysail with a WNW wind around 12 knots apparent. After an hour of perfection, the winds began to gust to past 20 apparent, which would cause the boat to try and round up toward the wind with a heavy weather helm. This would last for about a minute, maybe three, then back off again to twelve knots. A heavy degree of weather helm tells me that I have too much mainsail set for the conditions. The problem with gusting winds is that if you trim for the gust, you leave a lot of speed rolled up on the boom in the longish lulls between gusts. I could ease the main and dump a lot of air with each gust, but this is not a way to spend an otherwise great night at sea. I decided then to reef the main and leave full headsails up. This worked so well that an hour later when the gusts seemed to build more often and with a little more force I double-reefed the main. I lost only half a knot, but gained a flat sailing boat with no more than a healthy touch of weather helm. I seemed to be learning to be a cruiser after all. Captain Doogie would be proud.

That night I made a huge bowl of red beans and rice and ate it in the cockpit. I was less than mile offshore trying to avoid the northbound current known as the Gulf Stream. The coastal traffic consisted primarily of moderate to large cargo vessels, and as twilight gave way to darkness, I became increasingly aware that I was in for a long night.

Near midnight I approached Ft Lauderdale with heavy eyes and a half-alert brain. Port Everglades is more than a departure point for tourist cruise ships. It is an active port that has more ship traffic than facilities to serve it. This can make for crowded conditions outside the harbor entrance.

Each time I leaned against the cabin trunk I would drop off to sleep only to bounce awake a few minutes later. This was bad enough, but my real concern was that my uneasiness might fade, and I would sleep too long. It would only take one time and my cruise could be over.

Large vessels have trouble seeing pleasure boats, especially when those vessels are in danger of being run down. The long, high bows of these ships make the effective range of visibility often more than a hundred yards forward of the leading edge. I once saw a cartoon in *Cruising World* that pictured a freighter tied to a dock. A Coast Guard officer asked

Raise the Sails

the captain if he had seen any sailboats during his crossing. The captain replied that no, he had seen none this trip. On the bow of the freighter, hanging from the anchor was a crushed sailboat with its broken mast dragging in the water. When I closed my eyes I pictured the name *Silk Purse* written across the stern of that sailboat.

It was time to become proactive as the business gurus are fond of saying.

"On the deck, sailor, and give me twenty!"

"Aye, Captain Oakley, sir!"

I dropped down on the deck and counted off twenty pushups then twenty deep knee bends and finished with twenty jumping jacks. Now I was awake. I took up my position on the helmsman seat right behind the wheel.

"Now, sailor, disengage that autopilot and sail your vessel like a man."

"Aye, Captain Oakley." I punched off the autopilot and assumed control of the helm. "Helm is under my hand, sir."

"OK, sailor, stay alert and at your post." By now I could visualize Captain Oakley again dressed in his 1825 Royal Navy uniform. "And don't make me come out here again!"

"I will remain alert, sir!" I sincerely hoped that he would stay in his cabin. I didn't much care for Captain Oakley any more than *Pequod's* crew approved of Ahab.

We sailed along for the next couple of hours, and managed with little difficulty to dodge a couple of oil tankers and a cruise ship of some sort. I was feeling alert and competent. It was still a long way before we reached the Keys where the vessels would be more our size, but we were doing well. I was confident that we would see the upper Keys by first light.

I awoke with a start from a drool on chin and chin on chest position still slumped in my helmsman seat. Was something wrong? I popped to attention and began a 360 check. To my immediate left was the stern of a freighter. Behind me, another was glowing with enough light to serve a small city. Behind me! If I were to back straight toward it, my stern would catch it amidships. How we missed being run down by both those ships I did not know. The immediate problem though was less than a hundred yards ahead. Rising from the water, almost higher than I was able to see, was a ship the size of Miami. It was ablaze with lights from stem to stern. We were so close to it that I couldn't tell if it was heading east or west, out of or into the harbor. What to do? Where the hell was Captain Oakley when you needed him?

I swung the boat's nose into the wind and centered the main down hard. The headsails flogged like they were coming apart. While I waited for the boat to lose way, I did a sloppy job rolling up jib and staysail. The depth sounder still read forty-five feet; we had a little room before we were near to a beaching. I punched the autopilot to life and made my way to the bow. Breathe slowly, you're OK, I told myself, as I stood ready to drop anchor. If nothing else, once anchored, I could wait until morning and figure all this out in the light. It would all make sense in the light of day. Right?

It was about then, just before the anchor splashed, that I noticed that none of the vessels had their steaming lights on. None had changed position relative to me. Finally, I remembered the ship's anchorage a bit north of the Port Everglades Inlet. If you go to Ft. Lauderdale Beach, you can see these ships anchored less than a mile off shore. No wonder I couldn't tell which way they were going; they were anchored.

I secured the anchor on my bow and went aft. I had the Yanmar fired up in ten seconds. We passed astern of the vessel I had almost T-boned a moment earlier. Once past her I turned east and we headed out to sea.

That was a near disaster and had only been averted because I woke up. What had caused me to bounce up fully awake with such timely fortune? The sails were as quiet as ever. The radio was silent. I resolved then to paint a large Chinese style eye on either side of *Silk Purse's* bow. However, I immediately realized that if she had been the one to wake me, painting the eyes on her bow was unnecessary. My boat could see in the dark, another hidden value built in by Island Packet.

The rest of the night I had zero problems staying awake.

A weak glow loomed in the eastern sky barely above the first evidence of a horizon. Moments later it became a pale orange aura spreading across a sea that gently turned from onyx to a hue resembling a slate and granite composite. Low clouds were painted with a dark brush, while the ones more overhead almost glowed in lighter shades, some almost white. Then the sea acquired an azure hue, and was mimicked by the sky. Though the splendidly incandescent dome of the sun had not risen from the Atlantic, I had the comfort that always comes with dawn at sea.

Time for Beethoven.

I put on the ninth symphony, and as the wan beginning of the sunrise shifted to a brilliant intensity, the music built toward its own crescendo. The choir sang Beethoven's *Ode to Joy*, and I sang along making up my own phonetic version of the lyrics.

Joy was what I felt. The night was over, and it had been a long one. I had more than dawn to celebrate. *Silk Purse* sailed in less than twenty feet of water. About a mile off my starboard bow, a radio tower rose from a small island that, if I proved to be any sort of navigator at all, must surely be Boca Chita Key. The island and the sunrise went so well with the music that I wondered if Beethoven had been sailing the Keys when he wrote it. A quick GPS check told me I was right on target.

Lesson: Those were freighters out there! The drill here is a reinforcement of Chapter Fourteen. Coastal cruising can be more dangerous than an ocean passage.

Corollary: While the bow first ramming technique is workable for a fleet of tiny fishing boats, the oil tankers of our lives must be dealt with differently.

Chapter 17: *Knockdown, Drag Out*

Not all the legs I sailed produced events that combined a degree of humor with an obvious lesson. By this time, many, actually near all, of the segments *Silk Purse* and I made were reasonable examples of how good fortune and preparation, combined for success.

After I verified my position as a bit northeast of Boca Chita, I had as good a sail as I ever experienced in the northern Hawk Channel heading south toward Tavernier. I met up with Trey and we spent two days in moderate debauchery. When he went to work, I went to Key West. After a few days spent in absolute decorum, I realized it was time to head for the Bahamas.

I sailed back up the Hawk Channel to Tavernier with a southwest wind and spent a pleasant night anchored on the west side of Marathon Key. From Marathon to Tavernier I didn't crank the engine. I decided that I might like to spend a day not listening to the Yanmar and resolved to anchor under sail.

After all, these waters have been sailed more years before the invention of the diesel than since. Blackbeard, Stede Bonnet, Calico Jack Rackam, and Woodes Rogers had no concept of an engine, and they sailed thousands of miles among the Keys and Bahamas.

These ghosts were scant company and no comfort. Where are you, Judi? That's right, I'm the one who left. Details, I hate when they conspire against me.

When I rounded Tavernier Key, I turned WNW to where I had seen a number of boats anchored a week ago. With hardened sail, I came into the anchorage close hauled. I rolled up the headsails and continued into the anchorage. As we neared a good location I centered the main down hard and turned the boat into the wind. *Silk Purse* lost way and slowed her to approach the key. I went to the bow and readied the Bruce. When it seemed I was in the perfect spot, I dropped the hook and I set on a short scope with the chain running under the keel. Slowly the boat swung around then back again nose to the wind. I let out more chain and *Silk Purse* seemed to hang on her chain alone. I went aft, released the main sheet and pushed out the sail backwinding it to give some momentum aft. Soon the *Silk Purse* backed or crabbed away from the anchor until the chain tightened and *she* swung back with her nose to the wind.

This was the first time I had anchored without the assistance of diesel power, and after a half-hour of wondering I decided to take a look at the anchor. I dropped the dink into the water, but left it on the davit lines. I had no plans to use it except to assist me in returning to the boat. It is no easy task for a swimmer in the water to climb up the five feet of hull and railings to *Silk Purse's* deck. I wasn't even sure I could do it. I grabbed mask and snorkel and launched myself into the water. We had anchored in ten feet of water, so less than a hundred feet ahead my Bruce should be buried in a sand bottom.

I kicked my way along the chain, which I could see perfectly in the vodka clear water. I saw no fish, but I did see one small ray snuggled on the bottom half buried in the sand. The chain was stretched out straight like it should be. A few more kicks and I could barely make out the shank of my anchor emerging from the sand. I did a little surface dive, thinking that I would pay a closer visit to the ray on my return trip.

Near the bottom, I made a U-turn and came face to face with the biggest permit I have ever seen. My reflex was to suck in a quick breath, and I got a mouth full of brine for my trouble. The permit is a cousin to the pompano and I wondered if this one didn't somehow know about all those relatives of his I had eaten cooked in one of those restaurant paper sacks. In a contest deciding who would be the diner and who would be the dinner, I didn't like my odds. Fortunately the permit was more curious than hungry. Plus my reaction scared him almost as much as he did me, and with a flick of his tail he was gone.

Back at the stern of my boat I dragged myself into the dink, stood up to lower the swim ladder, and climbed back into the cockpit. A quick shower at the helmsman seat and I was secure and feeling no worse for the incident. I did resolve though, that should I ever tell this story, the permit would become a shark, but, as fortune dictates, this is a non-fiction book.

Lesson: The lesson here has something to do with the guy who couldn't back his boat from the slip is sailing alone and anchoring under sail. If he can do that, anyone's dream can become reality.

The Great Bahama Bank is an underwater plateau that rises more than a mile from the floor of the Atlantic to just below the surface at high tide. It extends southeast from Miami for some three hundred miles almost to Cuba. (Cuba: A large and beautiful island filled with wonderful people that we would benefit from knowing.) The Northwest Providence Channel separates the Great Bahama Bank from the Little Bahama Bank (Remember the Abacos?).

Bimini rises from the western most edge of the Great Bahama Bank and that is where I chose to clear customs and spend my first couple of nights in the Bahamas. My next stop would be Nassau, New Providence Island, where I was to meet Doug and his wife to be, Jane. It would be good to have crew on board to share in the sights and later the memories.

Solitude, since Judi left a few weeks ago, had lost much of its appeal. I had to be on constant watch for the blues and the family visiting uncle, depression. It is not as though I dreaded my own company, but a journey like this made alone—something is missing. Already there had been so many times on this trip when I had wanted to punch Judi in the ribs and shout: "Look!" But there was no one there. I had sailed away from wife, what family I had, and life-long friends.

Escapism, wish for it at your own peril. Do you see how the blues can sneak up on you?

So I resolved to trade the simplicity of Bimini for the buzz of Nassau. I had heard in a song sometime before that Nassau had gone funky. Maybe the sounds of Nassau would drive the blues away. Let's get funky with it then.

There are at least two ways to get to Nassau from Bimini. The first (taken by almost everyone) is across the bank where one is in shallow and somewhat protected waters. It is possible to anchor if you get sleepy. It is also possible, though not likely, to run into one of the navigation lights. These lights are notorious for being out and thus as much an aid to navigation as a sand trap is to par. The second route is the one I chose. It takes the venturesome sailor north from Bimini across the top of the bank in the Northwest Providence Channel. After rounding the Berry Islands, it's a straight blue water shot to Nassau.

My route is longer, but since I will sail all night, it takes less time. It all depends on what you prefer: an all night sail in relatively deserted waters or a sleepless night in a choppy anchorage. The truth is I wanted to do a different sort of thing for whatever twisted reason.

I left Bimini around 0900 and cleared the channel without incident. *Silk Purse* and I motored north in a dead calm until I believed we could cut the northwest portion of the bank and save a few miles. When we took up a course of 100° magnetic, we also picked up a southwest wind. With batteries on full charge, I raised the sails and doused the engine, which is one of the most gratifying catharses imaginable (I keep telling you that, so it must be true). A couple of minutes later, we were cruising on a broad reach at a little over seven knots.

I rounded the Berry Islands in pitch dark and turned south. The wind went dead calm again. With headsails doused and Yanmar humming, I continued south toward Nassau. I wasn't sailing, but I was grooving. Time for Jimmy Buffet. A few minutes later and I was singing at the top of my voice about mother, mother ocean.

Raise the Sails

Log Entry: 0145 Wind building from west to 12 apparent—sailing

Log Entry: 0230 wind NW 17 apparent, reefed main.

Before I left Bimini I was able to get a clear weather forecast that mentioned a cold front stalled over Jacksonville, Florida. I surmised that the front must now be on the move toward Nassau and accompanied by a serious squall line. Now, in the black western sky I could see the frequent looming of heat lightning painting clouds with gold and red. These were followed by jagged bolts of electricity accompanied by the deep rumble of thunder. Seas were still less than five feet and the wind was holding steady from the NW at less than twenty apparent. I reefed the main again and we continued toward Nassau at well over 8 knots. At this rate I would be outside the harbor well before dawn.

By 0300 the wind was gusting past 30 knots and it was time to get some if not all the jib furled. I left the helm on auto and headed for the roller furler line, but my tether was too short to allow me to reach the gear. I broke my cardinal nighttime rule and unsnapped the tether from my harness.

This in itself is a dangerous and foolish thing to do. At night on a brisk sea to fall overboard is a death sentence. Even if there is a well-experienced crew onboard a sailor overboard is as good as dead. This is something that had been programmed into my brain since I began thinking of a sailboat, so what came next is hard to understand even as I sit here doing rewrites.

Instead of cranking in the furling line to tame the jib, I found myself standing high on the weather rail. The wind gusted in my face as I hung one handed from a shroud and swung against the lifelines.

"Come on, come on."

I stepped over the lifeline and screamed a curse at the wind. I could do it right here, and nobody would know. It would be an accident.

"Come on. No one will know but us."

The wind gusted and there was a little spray. Or was it rain. I felt my foot teetering on the cap rail. So easy. So quick. Just step off the rail.

"Come on, come on. You know what to do."

"Go to hell!" I know I said this out loud.

A moment later I was back in the cockpit reattached to my harness wondering what had just happened, or what had not taken place. Was I really about to do it? Was Old Scratch close to taking possession of what he had claimed as his so long ago? I did not know then and do not today. It is hard to believe as I sit and write this that I would do something so stupid as stepping over the lifelines in that weather if I had not been serious about the next step.

Back in the cockpit I resisted the urge to unhook again and instead extended my tether to its full range. This late, this tired, and this messed up, I didn't attempt to muscle the furling line in, but put it on the winch straight away. I began cranking in the headsail when it became apparent my excitement for the evening was to continue. I will report what follows as clearly as I can recall it.

I was on one knee cranking in the genoa. The jib sheet was in my left hand and I was allowing it to slip pretty much without resistance through my fingers. This is done so that the sheets don't flay about and become tied in knots as you may remember they did on the Savannah trip. The wind continued to howl in the rigging, but we were OK, and I felt in no jeopardy.

Raise the Sails

To this day I am not sure why, but I looked to windward (starboard) in time to see a wall of water where two minutes ago the seas were five feet tops. The water was darker than the night around me and rose as far as I could see. It was on me in an instant. It lifted *Silk Purse* straight up what seemed like ten feet, and then unceremoniously slammed her on her port side.

It is difficult to describe the exact motion of the boat, because I was washed sprawling from the starboard side across the cockpit like a starfish caught in the surf. I remember the wheel seemed to be somehow upside down as I tumbled past it. Seawater engulfed the cockpit, but I can't say how high it came over the rail. I continued to careen over the port coaming until my head was between the port lifelines and thrust into the sea. I was stopped short of overboard by my harness and tether. That uncomfortable device I had rejected a few minutes before is responsible for my being here to record this today. I suppose you may thank or curse it yourself depending on your opinion of the writing.

An instant later *Silk Purse* was back on her feet and sailing as if she didn't remember a thing. A quick compass check and I find we are still on course, while I stood knee deep in seawater wondering what the hell had happened. Had I been about to step off the boat? Again, I wasn't sure then; I'm not sure now.

What had happened second? I am not sure of that either. My best guess is a waterspout. I believe there was too much energy in that wall of water to have been a rogue wave. By the time I thought to look there was no wall of water in my limited sight distance. My subsequent log entry mentions a <u>heavy</u> wind, but I can't really say now that I noticed any more wind than was already gusting immediately before or after the incident.

What I do know is that I almost stepped off *Silk Purse's* starboard side and then almost immediately was nearly washed off her port side. I suppose that coincidences occur, but I have never thought them prevalent. Had this been a lesson? If so who had prepared it? From where had it come?

I worked my way forward and inspected the sheets. Oh yeah, they were tied in knots resembling hacked up cargo netting. As best I could tell all else was well. I rolled the jib as tight as I could and secured it with a piece of line.

Below decks, water sloshed on the low side of the aft cabin and in the main salon. The nav table had dumped open and tossed its contents everywhere. There was gear and stores dumped out of the floor locker in the galley. I checked the bilge. It was sloshing a bit more water than normal, but nothing major. I inspected my batteries, and they were secure and dry. All things considered we were relatively dry below. That is because I had two hatch boards pinned in place and the hatch cover had been locked back when the seas boarded us. I still had my cockpit cushions because I had tossed them below when I first thought the front was coming through. I was pleased that a lot of the things we talked about were in place when I needed them.

I pulled off my wet clothes and as I stood naked in the main salon I wondered if all the brine that filled my jeans was from the sea, or if I had gotten more excited than I realized. It was hard to tell and I was not surprised to realize my bladder was empty.

I got into some dry clothes and sat down at the nav station to make a log entry. After half a sentence, my hand was shaking too much to write.

Raise the Sails

I greeted the following morning with great anticipation. I had been hanging around outside Nassau Harbor since sometime before dawn. When the sun did finally rise, it loomed up from the ocean into a thick soup of fog. There was no sensation of light, more an absence of darkness as visibility improved but marginally. I eased toward where my GPS told me the harbor entrance could be found, but I could only see a hundred feet or so in front of my bow. I picked up my air horn and periodically squeezed off a warning of one long closely followed by two short blasts. I think that's the right signal—the idea is to make noise.

It was at this point in time that I realized that I was mimicking much of my life to date. Sitting in the fog while blasting away with the horn made me feel a little safer. However, I was avoiding the solution to my problem. Not far away a safe harbor waited. If I would stop whistling in the dark and face my situation, maybe I could find the entrance. I picked up the diesel to a little over 2000 rpm.

Soon I could barely make out the rise of the Island and even a couple of buildings in front of me, but the harbor entrance markers remained hidden. I continued forward until a dark object rose from the sea ahead. To port and still closer to shore, I saw a similar shape in the water. What I could see were several small freighters waiting as well. The morning remained dressed in mist and gloom, and I had no wish for any excitement entering Nassau Harbor. Seas were 8-10 feet and irregular. Unwilling to remain in the toss of the sea, I decided to work my way as close to what should be the entrance as possible and wait to follow one of the freighters in. This proved to be a good idea, since I made the entrance and was quite close before I could see the markers.

Once inside the harbor, I cruised the anchorage areas intending to find a premium spot to anchor and sleep off the evening's excitement. The premium spots were all taken, as were the not so premium spots. I dropped the hook in a spot close to or possibly in the main channel and was promptly instructed to move by Harbor Control.

Following that forced move, I attempted to anchor no less than eight times in three different spots. Eight times I dropped the anchor and eight times we drug through the harbor like a demolition derby team. Eight times I pulled up that chain and somewhere between the fifth and sixth time it got heavy. It also got long because I kept trying to set the Bruce on longer and longer scope.

Then Richard came over to my aid. He drove his dink all the way across the harbor and tied up to my stern without a word. He climbed aboard while I was in the midst of hauling in the anchor for the eighth time.

"Looks like you could use some help," he said. "I had the same trouble the other day. Why don't we put you on the hurricane chain?"

The harbor here is notorious for poor holding and hurricanes do visit occasionally, so the folks in Nassau have stretched a couple of chains across the bottom of the harbor and anchored them in cement. Tie off to one of these chains and you're not going anywhere.

"I still got a marker on the one right behind us, mon." He smiled and showed a mouth of white teeth contrasted against his dark skin. "Drive me over and I'll dive you line down."

"Deal." I said.

I would be less than honest if I didn't tell you that I was wondering what all this would cost me. I had heard the horror stories of Nassau and how no one there was to be trusted.

Before I had time to worry too much, he had my line and dove it down to the chain. A minute later he tossed me my other end and I tied off.

"What build of boat is this?" He asked climbing back on board.

"Island Packet," I said and tossed him a towel. "What do I owe you for the help?"

"You cannot pay me, mon." He shook his head in a manner that left no room for argument.

I did get him to stay a while that morning, and before he left I persuaded him to take a bottle of chardonnay. Richard was my first contact in Nassau, and he set the tone for the several days that I was there. After Doug and Jane joined me the next day, we had a lot of contact with the citizens of Nassau, and were unable to find one that deserved their poor reputation. Nassau, like other "big" cities, is filled with busy people, who, despite their apparent haste, are as willing to befriend a polite stranger as we are ourselves. However, that is a story for another time.

Lesson: Living on a boat away from the shelter of the ICW requires a total immersion in the weather. It is an environment that cannot be escaped. Be a Boy Scout and always be prepared for the weather. I would have been better off had I waited on the front and followed it down. Though it would not have prevented my knock down, I would have also been better off with the genoa furled early.

Lesson: Mental health, nurture it. Don't leave home without it or a keeper.

Chapter 18: *Enroute*

We (for the next couple of weeks, we no longer means *Silk Purse* and me, since Doug and Jane joined me in Nassau) approached Staniel Cay from the Exuma Bank with the late morning sun almost straight overhead. According to my guidebook and trusty charts the approach to Staniel Cay was straightforward. That proved to be the case, and we dropped the main near the Staniel Cay Yacht Club. A few minutes later we picked up a mooring about fifty yards off the Club Thunderball dock.

The club is named for the Thunderball Grotto where part of the James Bond film Thunderball was filmed. Thunderball Grotto is a large stone dome that encloses a space half filled with seawater. It is best to visit the site at low tide when the current is still and the water level is low. Naturally, we arrived on a falling high tide. This required a surface dive of several feet and a short underwater swim against a brisk current ripping through one of the entrances to the cave. Once I fought down a natural panic tendency that I experience anytime I enter an underwater cave, entry proved much easier than I had imagined. A few seconds after diving through the entrance, we surfaced in a surrealist dreamland of stone, water, and brilliantly colored fish. Irregular gashes in the dome sent brilliant shafts of light through the air and water, creating an inverted image of the dome on the sugar white sand floor. On the southwest side of the cave a substantial shelf rose less than a foot above the water's surface. Diamond drops of water sparkled all around it, and I half expected to see a mermaid basking within my grasp.

The cave and the area outside have been established as a marine park and are protected from fishing. A dive to a depth of less than ten feet brought me in contact with several Nassau grouper, a couple of lobsters, and one lemon shark. The shark, if viewed from a boat, would look to be about six, maybe seven, feet in length. A face-to-face encounter through a few feet of clear salt water had the odd effect of making the shark look like a twenty-foot eating machine. You can't possibly imagine the relief that surged over me when its next likely meal proved to be a school of yellowtail snapper swimming ahead.

Soon after Grotto Thunderball, it was time for Club Thunderball. That's when I first met Ruth. She had dark skin with honey toned highlights, a rare, big ivory smile , and a musical voice that she did not expend on idle talk. Her manner indicated that she had already heard enough BS from visiting cruisers to last her a lifetime, but that rare smile promised a good nature to the patient visitor. She collected our money for the mooring, opened several Kalick beers for us, and clued us in on the activities we could expect on Staniel Cay. By Exuma standards, Staniel Cay is a budding metropolis and boasts the largest population between Nassau and

Georgetown. I don't know how many people live on Staniel, but fifty seems right.

"You get a lot of sharks out there in the harbor?" I asked Ruth as she slid a pair Kalicks to Doug and me.

"Just some babies now and then," Ruth said and turned her attention to the squawking VHF that lived under the bar.

"Club Thunderball, Club Thunderball." It was Jane's voice spilling from the radio. She had remained on the boat and I was willing to bet she was tired of awaiting Doug's return.

"Thunderball back," Ruth spoke into the mike.

"Have you got two boys up there trying to drink all your beer?"

"I got a couple here." Ruth smiled and looked our way.

"They claim to be brothers, but I don't know."

"Well, if they're both gray-headed, send them back to the boat while they can still drive the dinghy."

"We do that—Thunderball out."

We finished the beers and settled the check. As we started for the door I turned and caught her eye.

"That wasn't a baby shark I saw this afternoon. Looked more like Jaws to me."

"How big?" Ruth looked at Doug for confirmation.

"He told me it was as big as the boat," Doug said. "But I didn't see anything, so I wonder what he saw."

I scratched the side of my face with my middle finger extended solo. That well-known signal demonstrated my degree of respect for my loving brother.

"How big?" Ruth put a hand on her ample hip and gave me a head-shaking stare that demanded a realistic answer.

"Six feet, maybe seven," I said.

"Uh-uh, more like four, maybe five." Her face broke into a smile. "That's Jimmy, he cruises through here every day.

Raise the Sails

Don't you be scaring that boy. He's more scared of you, than you're scared of him."

After two nights swinging on the Club Thunderball mooring, we headed toward Georgetown. Half way down we decided that we should anchor up in a secure spot and wait out the cold front that was rumored to be on the way. We would need an anchorage protected from the west winds that announce the arrival of such fronts. After some inspection of our charts, we found the perfect spot and spent the night in beautifully deserted water protected by several cays near Lee Stocking Island. We had an early meal and turned in for a much needed rest.

Sometime in the middle of the night, all three of us were awakened by cannon blasts of thunder as the storm hit. We converged in the main salon wiping sleep from our eyes.

"We need to catch some of this rain," I said, pulling out two plastic covered throwable cushions.

"Yeah," Doug agreed. "But let it wash the salt off first."

I was topside in a flash with a bottle of shampoo, waiting for what I hoped would be a long sustained downpour. The rain hit us before the wind did, which is a general indication that we are in for a good blow and a lot of fresh water falling like manna from the sky.

"All right!" Doug danced on one foot waiting for the shampoo. "It's going to be a good one."

It was. We all three luxuriated in the cool fresh water as it washed salt off *Silk Purse's* decks and rehydrated skin that had been in a salt environment long enough to spawn dreams of freshwater swimming pools. We danced around like three kids on an overpriced slip-and-slide, miles from civilization.

"I'm catching some of this." I went forward and placed the two throwable cushions below the water fill pipe. They would act as a dam and cause the rainwater to pool up at the water fill inlet. "All right!" I pumped a fist in the air and opened the cap. Fresh water funneled into my thirsty tank below.

"Please tell me that's the water fill—"

"Yeah, Bro. I checked it three times before I opened it." That was true, but still momentary panic gripped my throat and squeezed, as I aimed the flashlight beam back on the opening. It said water, not diesel, and I could breathe again. "How much you think we'll get?"

"No clue." Doug shrugged and went back to the cockpit to play on the slip-and-slide.

I watched as water ran off the doghouse, down the side deck, and into my water tanks. I was happy because before we left Nassau I filled up the diesel and the water tanks. We held $41.50 worth of diesel; the water cost $46.00. I told you; sailors are cheap.

That night it rained and blew like stink until the early morning hours. I opened a bottle of cabernet and drank it as I watched the needle on my water gauge edge its way to past three-quarters full. My estimate is that we collected about sixty gallons that night.

The sail to George Town the next morning was among the best I have ever experienced. We broad reached over a polished lapis lazuli sea often punching the knot meter well past 9 knots. Call Doug and ask him if you don't believe me.

Lesson: In a remote local, wealth is more accurately measured in terms of usable commodities such as fresh water and diesel fuel. Soon I would have other lessons on wealth and values.

Chapter 19: *Mecca*

Silk Purse pointed her nose directly along a line extending from the top of Industry Hill over Smith Cays and out to the Exuma Sound. We beat into about fifteen knots of apparent wind on a course of 200° M. Once through Conch Cay Cut, we turned southeast, then back south and slowly worked our way into Elizabeth Harbor. This is the famed anchorage for the settlement legendary among cruising sailors and absolute Mecca for eastern U.S. cruisers. George Town, Exuma.

One of the attractions is the harbor itself. Elizabeth Harbor is huge. The day we arrived there were approximately 150 boats at anchor, and the harbor easily had room for 350 more. Some of the old time visitors to George Town are likely to disagree with this assessment claiming that the 150 is vastly over crowded. We were first time visitors and the harbor hardly seemed over crowded to us.

Even today it is possible to find that secluded spot among the small cays and rocks that are sprinkled throughout the harbor. About one nautical mile north of George Town along Stocking Island you will find Hamburger Beach, Volleyball

Beach, Anchoring holes 1, 2, and 3 as well as multi-hull hole. During peak season you can expect to find beaches teaming with activity and a very social cruiser's community. Across the harbor, between Moss Cays and the channel leading into George Town, it is easy to anchor and it's a short dinghy ride to town. Down near Red Shanks, Isaac Cay, and Crab Cay it is possible to escape the crowds.

We found our spot with room to spare off Moss Cays and near town. Once the hook was buried in the sandy bottom and *Silk Purse* was resting comfortably on her anchor chain, we splashed the dink and were soon tying up at the Exuma Markets dock.

All three of us were anxious to explore the settlement, each for our own reasons. Jane was intent on getting a feel for the history of the town and island. Doug had dreamed for sometime about visiting George Town. Like I said it *is* Mecca. As for me, my trip was a success the moment I set foot on the shore here.

All this being said, I was surprised at my reaction. After touring the market and one shop, I stopped at what for the next several weeks would become my hangout, the Two Turtles Inn. Doug and Jane went ahead and toured the town. I sat down to an unscheduled meal of rum and despair. Though neither dish I ordered up was agreeable in flavor, I gorged myself on one and washed it done with the other.

Perhaps it was my brother's happiness that brought my own condition into focus. Even though this was not the first time since my adventure began that my life had caught up with me, it was not a welcome visitor. The life I had left in the States was still there and still a mess. My business partner and I had parted ways, and I felt sure that we would be better off for the split. The problem of what I might do for a living was something I felt certain I could and would address once George Town was traded for Georgia.

But what would I do with the important part of my life. There was Judi; and all my instincts told me that a reunion was both possible and desirable.

Inside I felt empty or incomplete, like an electronic circuit with a vital part missing. I had a power source of sorts, and the wiring of the circuitry was in place. I even had a display screen, comprised of my brain, emotions, and self-regard. What was missing was the transducer, the element that gives an electric circuit its reason for existence.

One of the crucial systems aboard *Silk Purse* is that of the depth sounder, without which navigating the waters of the Exumas would be exceptionally difficult. The circuit for the depth sounder has a power supply in the ship's battery bank. A display screen beside the helm gives a readout of the water depth. The circuit running through the boat can be in perfect working order, but if there is no transducer in the form of an echo sounder then all of the rest of the system has no purpose. There will be no value on the display screen and no value to the circuit. Like more than a few others, I did not find meaning at the bottom of a glass of Captain Morgan. What I did find was a lobotomy of sorts, and a means, no matter how unhealthy, to put my thoughts on hold.

Raise the Sails

Doug and Jane stopped to collect their captain and we returned to the boat for dinner, but I couldn't stay there. Explaining that I understood a couple's need for at least some privacy, I took the dink back to the Two Turtles. By 2100 (9 p.m. lubber time) the bar was closing down, but there were still several demons I had not drunk into submission. This made the invitation from Benjamin, a local whom I had just met, sound enticing.

"Ya mon, we going to the Hillside Bar." Benjamin was all smiles with his Chicago Bulls hat on about half sideways. "It a jammin' place. You should come with us?"

He pointed to two or three other local guys who also seemed of a mind to become closer acquainted with Captain Morgan. The next thing I knew I had settled my bill, and the four of us headed toward this jammin' place a few hundred yards down the road. We strolled along the road and Robert, one of our troop, came up to me and put his arm next to mine elbow to elbow.

"Mon, you darker than me." He laughed and gave me a friendly shove on the shoulder. "How will things be for you in the States, when you get back darker than me?"

"How the hell can you tell who's darker?" I asked. "It's pitch dark out here—not a light for fifty yards."

"But how will things be for you?" He seemed more serious.

"Rough, I'll probably have to go on welfare." He didn't know how close to the truth that was.

"You better stay out that sun!" They all thought that was funny as hell and so did I.

We got to Hillside. It wasn't jammin', but it was open. I bought the first round, which I figured was the reason I was invited. The four of us and a half dozen other local guys were it. The only woman worked behind the bar, and she wasn't interested in doing any jammin'.

I was wrong though about why I was invited. After that first round, I couldn't spend another dime.

Time picked up speed over the next few days as my despair retreated to lick its wounds. The next thing I knew I was putting Doug and Jane in a taxi headed for the airport. I dinked back to *Silk Purse* certain that the blues would be waiting, but I was wrong. It was Mike and Teresa. You haven't met them yet, but you'll like them, I know.

They sat in their dink tied to *Silk Purse's* stern, apparently waiting for me.

"All right, company!" I smiled and waved. "Where's Elvis?"

"Back on the boat," Mike said. "He's been begging for sweets all day and we decided to split while he wasn't looking."

"Have Doug and Jane already gone?" Teresa shaded her eyes from the sun as she spoke. She sort of tilted her head back and looked toward me under the palm of her hand. "We thought that was you coming back, so we waited."

I smiled and did my "spaniel with bobbing head" imitation.

"We thought maybe you could come over for dinner this evening then we could go to Two Turtles for a couple. You could play with Elvis. He likes visitors."

"Sure." More head bobbing, careful not to pant. "Sounds good to me."

Elvis was their six-year-old basset hound, and quite a sailor in his own right. Like most hounds his toilet behavior left a little to be desired, but Mike had placed a square of AstroTurf well forward on their boat for emergencies. Elvis was a harbor favorite. He could frequently be seen clowning around on one of the beaches or asleep under a tree. If you drove your dink by his boat, he always barked a friendly greeting. Each evening just after sundown he serenaded the anchorage with his *Ode to Sunshine Lost*.

The three of them lived as happily as you might want to imagine on their catamaran, which they named *Stray Cat*. Teresa was about five seven, blonde, tan, and beautiful. For some reason, my memories of Mike are less vivid. What I do remember is that they took me under their wing for a few days, and my dependence on Captain Morgan for company decreased. One evening at the Two Turtles Inn, Teresa had my whole story. I think it took her about a half hour to extract all my secrets.

"Well," she looked at me and smiled. "The good news is that at least you know *something* is wrong. I think you already know what it is, but if not—you'll figure it out."

"Who said anything was wrong?"

"You did, body language." She pinched me on my arm then leaned against Mike's shoulder. "The minute we started talking seriously, you stopped staring at my boobs."

"Is that true, Mike?" I wasn't going to cop to this without a fight.

"I don't know," he said. "I was staring at her boobs."

It's true; all men are pigs.

A few days later Mike and Teresa sailed away to Cat Island. In a little over three weeks, I would sail to Cat as well, but I never saw them again. I have received Christmas cards featuring Elvis dressed as Santa, and Elvis dressed as a skier, complete with skies, poles and a mean visor.

The two Turtles continued to be my hangout. There were other places, but I liked the way the open-air bar sat out near the road in George Town. People would stop by chat a while, maybe have a drink, maybe not. During the NBA play-offs, a group of us met most every night to watch whatever game was on. One night I arrived early so that I could get a seat. I walked up to the bar and oreoed myself onto a stool. Roni, an island girl young enough to be my daughter, was there dressed in her Michael Jordan jersey, as she had been the night before and the night before that. Her coffee and mahogany skin was highlighted with mocha, and she wore her hair in small, tight braids that were long enough to pull back in a sort of ponytail. The effect was quite fetching, and I used to tease her about getting my almost shoulder length hair rowed just like hers.

"Well, tonight's the night," she said walking up to my stool.

She leaned over, pressed her lips against my ear, and bit me just short of real pain. Her moist, warm breath whispered a promise, and chills raced own my back. A moment later her hand raked my face, and she pushed herself onto my lap.

Well, that **could** have happened.

Instead, I looked her up and down.

"The night for what?" I asked.

"Oh you dreaming, now." Roni had evidently read my mind. "It's time to row your hair. Cost you drinks though."

"Seems like a small price to pay."

She began immediately and continued through the pregame show, the first half, the halftime show, and right on through Michael and his boys beating whomever they were playing. I think it was the Hawks. Roni finally finished, then took a look at her work. She didn't laugh, and I took that as a good sign.

She went behind the bar and emerged with a Budweiser mirror held up so I could inspect my new look. My gray and yellow hair stood out from my head in four to six inch, semi-tight braids. I looked like the Medusa had stuck her entire arm in a light socket.

"My God!" I gripped the mirror and jerked it around trying to find a reason to believe it wasn't me. "I look just like Buckwheat!"

"Buckwheat, my ass," she said. "You look like cream of wheat!"

That evening I went back to *Silk Purse* with a lingering smile. I tied off the dink, bounced up the ladder, and went below to have a second look at my new style. I snapped on the light in the aft head and saw an intruder gawking back at me from the mirror. A few seconds later and my own beamy face emerged from beneath a giant rag mop of gray and sun-yellowed hair. Turning my head and looking for my good side soon proved fruitless.

"If you aren't the most danged fool sailor I ever saw, I'll kiss a pig!" A pea gravel voice rasped from behind.

I spun around, but saw no one. I could swear the rum bottles rattled inside the booze locker.

"What are you looking for?"

Captain Oakley stuck his head out of the forward cabin. He seemed to have aged some since I last saw him. He had several days' growth of a graying beard, and for the first time his uniform looked like he had a hobo for a valet. His hands were rough with large calluses: the kind you get from working with cement or crawling over dirty gravel.

"You know where I am." He knuckled his forehead and disappeared.

He was right about that. I knew where he was and suspect that you might as well. I looked back at my 'do and noticed I was a bit more scruffy than cure dog. Tanned almost to a weak coffee tint with gray and brassy, once dyed hair that had been braided into a rat's nest, I hardly recognized myself. A sweat stained T-shirt and sun bleached tobacco colored shorts completed my look. How could the girls resist? Roni had experienced no problem resisting, but maybe she just didn't like white guys sun roasted to a medium brown. I'm sure that was it.

It was only a little later that I wondered what Rubicon had I crossed. What dye had been cast that had set what many would have thought to be a reasonably successful life on a course toward a lee shore anchorage? Had this been one of those things every one but I could see?

What zodiac sign had I missed? Had I followed the wrong star?

My father's face coalesced in my mind. He appeared first as he might have looked when I was small and my memories of him were unspoiled. Soon his face changed to the wrinkled and foul one it had become on his last night when his head rolled from that trashcan and stared at me.

When had he decided to become a drunk? When had he crossed his Rubicon? My guess was there had been no Caesar moment; there had been no line to cross. Day by day alcohol built one row of bricks higher on his cell wall. Day by day, excellence was eroded by a river of indifference that created a monument to apathy and escape:

Come on. Yeah, come on.

Our Legacy comes in diverse forms, and once again I learned we are not required to listen. That night I decided to forgive my father.

My time at George Town rolled on. I made friends with some of the locals and some of the cruisers. I even got a spear fishing lesson from Robert. All the time I had been in the Exuma Cays, I fished several times a week and managed to bag exactly two grouper. During Robert's lesson, I got two, weighing about four pounds apiece. Small, but all I could eat before they went bad. There is a secret to successful grouper spearing. If you're interested, go down to George Town. They might tell you.

Looking back on my time at Georgetown, I can tell you that it did not pair up with any of my mental pictures. At first I was sorry that we arrived weeks after "the season" had peaked. I kept wondering what I had missed. I knew that the cruiser's race and the Family Islands Regatta had managed to take place without our participation.

Several hundred boats had gone either back to the U.S. or on to more southern harbors before hurricane season began for real in a month or two. I had envisioned a more vigorous social life among the cruisers that might have been there in February, but had dissipated by our arrival in late April.

To say that my first impressions of Georgetown fell short of my expectations would be fair if not precise. I believe that Doug was also disappointed, not so much by what he found there, but by what he did not. We had spent so much time discussing the prospects of seeing our imaginary Georgetown that we gave ourselves little chance for an early appreciation of the real place.

I'm sorry that my brother didn't stay there long enough to get to know more of the locals. In another sense it was fortunate for me that he did not. Had Doug been there the whole time for me to focus on, I might not have reached out to the people that I did. Without my loneliness, I might have missed the people that today embody my memories of the real Georgetown.

Lesson: Occasionally, the Rubicon can be wide and shallow with no apparent current, and we find ourselves on the other side with no memory of a crossing.

Chapter 20: *Staniel Cay Back*

We (once again just Silk Purse and me) left Mecca in route back to Staniel Cay. Noon was still an hour away, but already the sun had heated *Silk Purse's* decks to the point bare feet were near impossible. The sky played a perfect mimic to the dark blue of the sea. A few palette-shaped clouds hung suspended in the sky above a group of cays to port and were shaded with splashes of cobalt and coral reflected from the water and pink beaches below.

I had tried to sail but the wind was light and moved the boat along at less than two and a half knots. I wanted to be certain that I reached the anchorage near Lee Stocking Island before darkness threatened, so the diesel chugged along, intruding on the beauty of the moment. When the following wind began to blow the exhaust fumes from the engine into the cockpit, it became time for action. I fetched up the cruising chute and inside an hour had it set. An hour to set a sail is ridiculous amount of time, but with my chute and the peculiar idiosyncrasies of the sock used to control the sail an hour solo isn't unreasonable. You might notice that this is the first time I have mentioned the cruising chute since that race to Savannah some months and miles ago.

With the sail at last set and the captain near exhaustion, boat speed did settle in at near six knots when the engine fell silent. I killed the autopilot. We would sail as it is meant to be with only the wind song in the rigging for company. An occasional touch to the wheel kept *Silk Purse* on course, as she basically steered herself toward our anchorage.

Within a couple of hours the wind began to pick up, and soon the breeze became a little too fresh for the spinnaker. After some effort, I got the chute bagged and working sails set. With fifteen to seventeen knots of apparent wind, *Silk Purse* broad reached well over 8 knots. Soon our waypoint was within a few minutes sailing and I could barely make out the break in the cays that would be the entrance to the same anchorage where we had collected rainwater a few weeks earlier. I dropped the sails and motored into the anchorage where it was almost dead calm. The afternoon heat had peaked ten minutes before I dropped the hook and my skin was drenched in hot sticky perspiration. There wasn't a dry hair on my head, and the deck felt like a South Georgia blacktop road, firing through the soles of my topsiders. If there had still been eggs on board, I would not have needed a skillet. Fried, over-easy, or scrambled I could have fixed them on the cabin top. Once the hook was set in about twelve feet of gin clear water, I climbed the bow pulpit and launched myself through the air. Thoughts of being anchored in the world's largest martini raced through my mind. I splashed into the harbor waters like a wounded whale. It wasn't gin, but it felt good. I dived deep, looking not for the bottom, but for the coldest layer of water I could find. A few minutes later and it was time to climb aboard and take a long shower, wasting sinful amounts of freshwater.

As soon as I got to the stern my problem became overwhelmingly apparent. Hanging five feet in the air above my head the dink swung from its davits. Worse still, the swim ladder was properly folded over the stern lifeline. There would be no getting on board from the stern. Neither the port nor starboard sides offered any hope. And you guessed it there was not another boat in the anchorage.

The bow was even higher above my head than the stern. There was, however, the anchor chain that dropped vertically from the bow to the bottom. Also, *Silk Purse* was made with a bobstay that extended from the leading edge of the bow just above the waterline to the bowsprit. So besides the anchor chain, I have a stainless steel rod angling up and forward to the bowsprit.

I pulled my bulk hand over hand and foot over foot up the chain until I could reach the bowsprit that doubled as an anchor platform. More problems. As on most properly equipped cruising boats, there are two anchors permanently mounted on *Silk Purse's* bow. This second anchor was a Danforth type, with a long metal rod to which are attached two sharp flukes. The flukes are designed to dig deep into the bottom and properly secure the vessel. They would also dig deep into the thigh, innards or, worse of any sailor foolish enough to impale himself on them.

Avoiding the Danforth meant climbing over the bow aft of the anchor chain. On try number seven or maybe it was number eight, I arrived at the bowsprit a foot or so to the rear of where the menacing anchor lurked. This was accomplished by wedging myself against the bobstay and the hull. Trouble was, I was stuck with my back against the hull and feet screaming for mercy against the bobstay. One hand held the anchor chain, while the other sort of groped the deck for a handhold. If you don't think this sailor was exhausted, then you have much too fine an opinion of my conditioning. I would rest here just a minute. It occurred to me that somebody ought to take a picture, but there was no one there.

My feet jammed against the bobstay rod hurt so bad that I was forced into action. With much reluctance, I let go the chain and swung my right hand toward the bowsprit and caught the bowpulpit on the first try. Soon I had both hands on the stainless tubing of the bowpulpit, one foot on the bobstay, and one foot arching up and missing the bowsprit. I managed to chin up and get an elbow over the lower tube. A few minutes later I collapsed in the cockpit. My arms shook from the exertion, and slowly the image that I had produced in my mind to motivate me to drag my overburdened rear end back on deck began to fade. I had conjured up an image of a cream-of-wheat skeleton, its fingers wrapped in a death grip around the anchor chain. My still corn-rowed hair was sun bleached a dingy, urine-yellow, and the gulls were using my skull for a roost. You would have climbed up the side of that hull, too.

The following morning, I left the anchorage, sailed on to Staniel Cay, and picked up the same mooring near Club Thunderball that we had used better than a month ago. Some time later I was to hook up with Trey and his wife, Jan. A good time waited there, but in the mean time I would bike the hills and trails of Staniel Cay and visit with whoever was talkative.

Club Thunderball, like many a Bahamian business in the out islands and cays, kept irregular hours. They were open when they were open, most days for cocktails (beer or rum) and dinner, some days for lunch, and never in the morning.

If you consider that most cruisers find it necessary to leave as early in the day as the tides will allow, it becomes understandable why people began to leave money with me to give to Ruth. Occasionally, I wasn't open either. I might have dinked over to the yacht club or gone fishing or be otherwise engaged in any number of serious pursuits. Sometimes I found money taped to the stern of the boat or in an envelope lying in the cockpit. So it was that every couple of days I would show up to Club Thunderball bearing proceeds from their enterprise. One particular day I arrived with a few dollars and Ruth (you might remember her as the boss lady of the club mentioned when I stopped here earlier) opened a Kalick and slid it across the bar toward me as I entered.

"More rents!" I waved the fistful of ones and fives in the air. I caught the beer in plenty of time; you can be sure of that. "Thanks."

"What are you doing here?" Ruth gave me one of her appraising looks, ever on the lookout for BS. "What are you doing?"

I stared at her and wondered what she meant. I said, "Bringing you some cash."

"Don't fool with me, boy. You know what I mean."
I didn't and said so.

"When are you going to go take care of what ever it is you're trying to hide from?"

A good question. An exceptionally good question. It was certainly a more direct question than I had asked myself, at least out loud. When was I going to do it? What was it I was running to avoid? Sailing to avoid. The sailing is an end unto itself. I played mental tape number three in the Sid Oakley

Self-Deception Series (coming soon via infomercial). I got lost in my thoughts and didn't answer Ruth.

"I'm asking when. I'll leave what up to you." She placed a hand on her hip and stared at me waiting for her answer.

"Well, I'm leaving the Bahamas in about two weeks to a month. After that?" I shrugged my shoulders.

"I'm asking when." She put her rent money in a Cohiba cigar box and folded her arms across her chest.

"I'll be home by the end of June."

Ruth treated me to a huge smile. "Drink that beer; I got another one here for you."

I haven't seen Ruth since I left Staniel Cay. There are a lot of cruisers stopping at Club Thunderball these days, and truthfully I wonder if she remembers me. But I know I will never forget her or her unexpected wisdom and focus on my life.

As far as what Ruth meant and what had made her ask that question, I had no idea then and have little today. In retrospect, I realize that in their own way others had asked that question of me. Certainly Teresa did during the time I shared with Mike and her. Back in Georgetown, when the locals and I were walking to that jammin' place, Robert had asked, "How will things be for you in the States, when you get back darker than me?"

Was there visible evidence of the turmoil inside? There must have been. Maybe I was like the kid in school with the "kick me" sign on his back. What I do know, whether fostered by Ruth's question or not, is that the following morning I awoke with a budding determination to live up to the timing I had given Ruth. My answer to her was that I'd be in Georgia by the end of June had been one of convenience. Now it was beginning to feel like a promise.

I ran the dink up Pipe Creek and exited the protected water through a small cut toward Exuma Sound. I anchored near a small reef, and then with fins, mask, and spear began a quest for the evening meal. My mind would not focus on finding a grouper, and when the fifth dive in this usually productive spot only turned up two small barracuda sightings, the hunt was abandoned. All I kept thinking of seemed to center on departure preparations. Did I have enough fresh water to get me to Nassau? Did I have enough diesel? What stops would I make on my way back that I had not made on the way down?

I tied the dink astern of *Silk Purse* and climbed up the swim ladder. Trey and Jan were due this afternoon or tomorrow, but as yet I had been unsuccessful raising them on the radio. I shucked my wet shorts, went below, and picked up the radio mike.

"*Tres Bien, Tres Bien – Silk Purse*" I released the microphone key and waited a minute or so. *"Tres Bien, Tres Bien"*

Still no response, but I decided to leave the VHF on in case they tried to reach me. A couple of minutes later I hear the radio come to life.

"Vessel Calling *Tres Bien*, please respond on 1–2." The voice didn't sound like either Trey or Jan, but they had friends traveling with them. I was surprised how excited I was by the response.

"*Silk Purse,* on 1–2" I waited for a response.

"Yes, this is *Storm Warning.* We spent last night next to *Tres Bien* in Waderick Wells. They were planning to leave later today for Staniel."

"Roger that *Storm Warning.* Are you headed for Staniel Cay? I could reserve a mooring for you."

"Negative that. Can you advise on Lee Stocking anchorage?"

I smiled at my thoughts. Could I advise? Of course I could; drop your swim ladder before diving in.

"Beautiful anchorage. You should get lots of privacy there—great holding."

Sometime after noon I heard Trey calling me on the radio. They were in a school of dolphin and wanted to make sure I had no dinner plans. Plans? Those guys hadn't been down here long enough if they were still talking about making plans.

Lesson: Wisdom from an unexpected source is no less sage. Selah!

Chapter 21: *Inflection Point*

Everyone's life has at least one before-and-after point, a time or event of such significance that our brains automatically file the other events in our lives as occurring before or after.

Over the next week, I cruised with Trey and Jan together with mutual friends, Bill and Jill until we reached Nassau. We would stay there a couple of nights or so while some shopped and others didn't.

Our last night together in Nassau Harbor was spent indulging in a splurge of beefsteak and cabernet aboard *Tres Bien*. Trey had taken a slip in a marina, and I had dinked over primarily to spend an afternoon planning our trip across the Bahama Bank and on to Florida under the cool blanket of his air conditioner.

I was not necessarily of a mind to leave in the morning. It was Trey who had a schedule. *Silk Purse* was in no hurry to exchange the freedom of open water and anchorages for the confinement of a slip back in the States. Though he felt a tugging to get home and begin anew a life interrupted, her captain was inclined to agree. The thought of returning to a life of structured productivity was no more appealing to me than docklines and shore power cords were to my boat. Ambivalence ruled my life, not a schedule. Still, there was Judi. We still had a chance; a chance I felt worth taking. Also, there was the matter of the commitment made back in Staniel Cay. While it did not loom large in my plans, still it was undeniably there. So I sat in the cool comfort of *Tres Bien's* main salon and used a brown-and-serve roll to mop up the remnants of the first beef I had tasted in weeks. I downed another glass of good cabernet and agreed to leave Nassau in the morning. Trey and Bill would sail to Florida, while their wives would fly home at first light tomorrow.

Assuming a reasonable forecast, we would leave in the morning as well. Outside the harbor it was blowing a good thirty knots, but things were predicted to settle down overnight to a fresh breeze in the early hours, finally dropping to around fifteen in the afternoon. If that proved true, tonight would be my last in Nassau. We would sail toward Chub Cay, then turn onto the bank and sail all night toward Cat Cay. I had never been to Cat Cay (as opposed to Cat Island) and was less than anxious to visit what promised to be an extension of Miami Beach. I envisioned obnoxious gold-chained power boaters in a contest to see who could be the loudest and most testosterone effusive. But stop there we would, and who knew? Maybe I would like it after all.

The following morning I arose early and rigged jacklines bow to stern on either side of *Silk Purse*, placed my harness and tether in the cockpit, and generally prepared the boat for an ocean passage. My memories of the seaway just north of Nassau, New Providence were mostly of the knockdown a few months before. While there was still a bit of a blow outside, there seemed little doubt to the weather prognosticators that things would lay down this afternoon as predicted. No repeat of our last situation was expected, but we would leave the harbor prepared under any circumstances.

By now it was 0800 and Trey and Bill finally had gotten their wives into a taxi headed for the airport and were backing *Tres Bien* from her slip. I raised and secured the anchor, then prepared to raise the main. We headed ourselves into the wind, and up went the main with two reefs in place as the autopilot kept us on course. The wind blew at near twenty-five true as we motor-sailed through the Nassau Harbor entrance. In spite of the brisk wind, I ran the Yanmar to charge my low batteries in the house bank. I could feel *Silk Purse* pleading for a little more sail so that she could charge ahead, a thoroughbred with the bit in her teeth. Well, maybe a Clydesdale.

North of New Providence the batteries were charged, and *Silk Purse* broad reached across eight-foot seas under a double-reefed main, staysail and a modest amount of genoa at a 7 knot pace. Ahead Trey was healed well to port with a full main and genoa and he was slowly drawing away from us.

"*Silk Purse.*" The radio squawked.

"Yep, we're awake," I answered on the handheld.

"You better put some more sail up and come on, if we're planning to make the Northwest Channel light before dark."

"We'll get there." He was making no more than a half-knot more than I was, and it hardly seemed worth it to spend the entire day heeled over on our ear. "I'm not racing you or daylight today. I was thinking a nap." The prospects of being awake all night seemed good, and I thought an early deposit in the sleep bank a good idea.

"See you at Cat." He said.

Less than an hour later I saw Trey had rolled in his genoa and set his staysail. His boat climbed off its side and they settled in a mile and a half or so ahead.

He was right though; we passed the Northwest Channel light in full darkness. This would have been absolutely no problem except it was out, as it is much of the time. Even at almost twenty-five feet tall, a dark light is of little use on a dark night. We both avoided a collision with the light and passed it to port without incident.

The wind had already dropped to about 17 apparent, when we turned west across the bank. I jibed the boat to port tack, let out all my genoa and broad reached in complete silence across the less than two-foot rollers over the bank. I rolled along at 7 knots or better and saw no reason to shake out a reef.

For a while, I could see the warm glow of *Tres Bien's* lights ahead. But I had little interest in following too closely. The sky was almost completely clear of the day's heavy clouds and I remembered I had two fresh grouper steaks in the refrigerator. I turned on the gas grill that was bolted to my stern pulpit and went below to season the fish. I would have grilled fresh grouper in copious quantities with whatever vegetable was below. Add a glass of chardonnay to this and I would be in heaven.

A pound of grouper and a few black beans later, I was wishing that I had managed to save a little more wine than the less-than-full glass that I found. But the stars were out in full force. I shut off all lights on the boat, killed the stereo, and stretched out in the cockpit. Silence. All I could hear was silence. Not even the sea made a sound as *Silk Purse* ghosted across the calm waters of the Bahamas Bank.

Sid Oakley

It felt like I was sailing through the stars themselves as the junction between the sea and sky became obscure. Time seemed to evaporate on the warm air that bore us away, and at that moment I cared little if we reached our destination or sailed on forever. In fact *Silk Purse* was so pleased on this point of sail that she required only the occasional touch to the wheel to keep her happily on course. Somewhere over the Bahama Bank, my anxiety about returning stateside began to dissipate. I was going home, going to take care of whatever it was that Ruth was talking about when we last spoke back at Staniel Cay. I was going home to Judi.

It was then that I heard it for the first time. Not a voice like someone speaking aloud, but clearly and more in the manner of a song you hear in your mind. You are acutely aware that only you hear the sound of Beethoven, Steely Dan, or Bob Marley, but hear it you do. This was like that only more so.

What I heard with a clarity and persistence that would not, could not be denied, was a voice repeating the same phase again and again.

"You're coming home to me too, Sid".

Yeah, that's what you think. I sat up straight and shook my head, but this wasn't a single hander's hallucination. I saw nothing, and again this was in my head, hanging there similar to a Stones guitar lick series, but stronger, clearer. My sailboat theme song had never played so clearly in my mind. This wasn't Henry Mancini.

"You're coming home to me, Sid."

I went below. The radio! That's it. I left it on, and that sorry Trey is messing with me. The radio was off, so was the stereo.

"You're coming home. You're coming home to me, too."

OK, now I knew what it was. I was going nuts. And why not? I had been talking to an apparition in the form of an old sea captain for the better portion of a year. Hadn't I screwed up every relationship I'd started? All of them? Hell, yes! Even back to high school when I had screwed up things with God. God? Talking to me? Not a chance.

"Hell, yes!"

OK, I know what you're thinking. If this were a courtroom scene from the television, the DA might stride back and forth in front of the jury box for a moment then stop and lean on the rail. With his head cocked and brow wrinkled into his best look of bewilderment he would address the jury.

"Ladies and gentlemen." He rubs his chin and shakes his head at an angle. "How many hallucinations is this guy planning to conjure up? I know we would like to believe him, but please! We've had a pretty steady diet of this Captain Oakley. Then we get Satan sitting cross-legged on his chest. Now, he hears from none other than God himself. Who might we next expect to appear, Peter Pan?"

In the defense of my credibility, I can only offer that I was never certain that Captain Oakley was actually on *Silk Purse* with me. You suspected as much. Didn't you? Satan was always there, but he was a devil of my own creation.

God? I believed it then. I testify to it now.

As for Peter Pan, I refer you to the DA.

Whether it was Him or not, I thanked God that the voice in my head stopped. The rest of the evening went quietly and in a normal fashion. I turned on the stereo and listened to Bob Marley. I knew Bob wasn't God, but then he didn't sound at all like the voice I had heard inside my head, either.

The next thing I knew the sun was peaking over the horizon at my back. On the horizon ahead, I saw Trey's boat and the outline of what must be Cat Cay.

I turned on the VHF.

"*Tres Bien, Tres Bien.*" I spoke into the handheld.

"Where have you been?"

"Back here, I had the radio off."

"Well, I've got an overheating engine, but we're right here at the entrance to Cat."

"Need help? I can anchor and dink over to you."

"No, we can sail in with the jib only and save the engine to dock with."

An hour later both our boats were tied up in a slip. I was pretty certain *Silk Purse* would have been happier in the Gulf Stream, but I was interested to see if I would hear the voice while ashore.

There was a buffet that night at the Cat Cay Club and we spent the evening there. The following morning we left headed for the Gulf Stream. I had heard no voice that night at Cat Cay, but then it would have been hard to hear anything over the rum, the band, and the Jimmy Buffet tapes.

Both our boats went through Gun Cay Pass located a few hundred yards north of Cat and a few south of Gun Cay. When the depth sounder told me I was in water too deep to measure, I turned west and let the Gulf Stream push me toward the Lake Worth Inlet. Trey and Bill made as much progress south as the current would allow. A couple of hours later my last radio conversation with them confirmed that their engine was running well and that they were confident of getting home to Tavernier Key.

Silence settled over *Silk Purse* as we rode the wind and current much as the mariners had hundreds of years before overheating engines were a problem. My mind, now with few distractions, soon returned to that night of sailing across the Bahama Bank, and to the voice I had heard so clearly in my skull. I waited for a repeat, but there was none. The sun rose to full vertical, and I went below to slap together a sandwich. Careful to avoid the voice of the whiskey bottle or even a can of beer, I came back with a cup of black beans and a Gatorade. My head needed to be clear in case the voice returned.

For days I waited to hear it again as I slowly made my way up the Florida coast. We entered the Lake Worth Inlet and spent two nights at the Old Port Anchorage. Then I spent two nights visiting friends in Stuart, Florida, followed by two nights on a mooring at Vero Beach.

Silk Purse and her sun-darkened captain continued up the ICW to a spot known commonly as Dragon Point. The point is the southernmost tip of Merritt Island and takes its name from a huge dragon that has been semi-famous for years. I anchored and waited. No voice.

I didn't tell Trey and Bill that night at Cat Cay Club about my experience the night before. To do so would have been totally out of place. They would have thought me crazy then, as possibly you do now.

That evening continues to have special significance for me, which I will attempt to explain. I have always thought that every life has at least one before-and-after point.

These are landmark episodes in our lives that are of such significance that our brain automatically files other events in our memories as before or after these points in time. So far, I can identify three from my life: before or after my marriage, before or after my mother's death, and before or after I began sailing. I'm willing to bet that most of us can put a finger on our before-and-after points with only a modest investment in soul searching.

Sometimes there are other, different times or events in our lives that are even more significant. An incident when something touches us, a time not unlike our before-and-after points, yet certainly more profound. I speak of an event that not only changes the way we remember things, how we file them away, but also how we perceive them. Our point of view was changed, transformed after this point in time.

Do me a favor; I don't believe I've asked for one yet. At the end of this section put the book down and think about a time when something outside yourself influenced your life to such a point that, after this encounter, your life was never the same. From this point on your life assumed a new direction. You understood things from a different perspective. A different set of rules and values came into play. At the time, like myself, you may not have understood the significance of the event. This point might have begun in failure or tragedy, but viewed in the context of your history, your life began with a new significance. This is what I have decided to call an inflection point. The inflection point in my life occurred one night on the Bahama Bank somewhere between the fall of darkness at the Northwest Channel Light and sunrise in sight of Cat Cay. I have come to believe that all of us can have an inflection point in our lives. It is required that we take a chance that they are real.

Somewhere sailing across the shallow, still waters of the Bahama Bank my spirit was reconceived. Much as my original conception in my mother's womb caused her little immediate, noticeable change, I experienced no extraordinary metamorphosis. There was no epiphany of understanding. If anything I was more confused than ever. However, since that evening

Raise the Sails

I have experienced a radical shift in perception. Personally, my appearance is much the same. I have the same southern drawl to my speech, and I still could lose a pound or two. Nonetheless, my universe is governed by a different set of laws.

I can imagine the shock those early to middle sixteenth century astronomers must have felt when they at last realized concepts cherished for centuries were false. How complete must have been their bewilderment when they began to understand that the earth was not flat. The radical, almost heretical theory that the earth revolved around the sun was probably true! Still, nothing had changed. The realization had caused no noticeable alterations to the environment. To all appearances the sun continued to rise in the east and set in the west. Yet, everything had changed. There was a new frame of reference.

Like others before me, I have come to realize that I was ambushed by grace. A God, that in my consciousness, had receded into a shadow of a concept and was but a glimmer of an intellectual possibility, had become manifest in my life.

One more point, and then, back to sailing.

If you have read any science fiction at all you are familiar with the idea of a domed city. The Founding Fathers, in their desire to protect the city inhabitants from all harm and taxing thought, built a dome that covered everything they considered worthwhile or essential. The weather is predictable; disease is shut out. The environment is sealed tight against intrusion by anything untoward, be it invading insects or a malicious thought. It seldom takes the reader long, however, to realize that life under the dome is less than it was advertised to be. While much adversity is eliminated, the people within the dome are incomplete. They are somehow less than whole because the dome has kept an essential part of them at bay. Their natural interchange with the world around them has been shut off. There is no umbilical cord linking them to it. Over time they have begun to think of the entire universe as being contained under the dome.

The people for the most part are unaware of their condition. It is only when the dome is pierced and fulfillment enters that their lives can become whole again. That night on the Bahama Bank the sphere that encircled the context of my life was pierced and something more came in. Something More was revealed to me.

Today, I trust that it was God because then I took a chance that it was God. In order to grasp the shift in my thought process, it is important that you realize that I did not then, nor do I today, understand either what happened that night or the growing faith I enjoy today.

Understanding in a "take it apart and see how it works" context might not be possible. Accepting that is a very difficult step to take for someone like myself. My thought process has always been of the classical 'if A equals B, and B equals C, then A equals C' type. This is a good approach for geometry, but when I attempted to analyze my Bahamas Incident in this manner, it fell short.

Imagine a blank piece of paper. Somewhere below its center a bold, horizontal line is drawn dividing the page in two. For the purpose of our discussion, let everything below the line represent our universe, the world we live in. Below the line time exists together with mortal man. Anything in our universe we are capable of understanding, even if that understanding requires a millennium of inspection.

Above the line is what I have fumbled to call the More. It is the domain of God who inhabits eternity. We are not equipped to understand anything above the line. The very concept of eternity defies my ability to describe it without using the finite terms of time and the limits of space. For me at least, it is not sufficient to define one thing as the absence of another. The concept of infinity defined in terms of the lack of boundaries fails to bring me clarity. If the universe is expanding constantly, as many scientists will tell us, I cannot define whatever it is into which the universe is expanding. I have no problem with planets, solar systems, and galaxies making up a universe of which we are an infinitesimal part. I even have a crude understanding of black holes. But how can the universe have no end? If it does have an end, then what is on the other side of its boundaries? A void, a vast nothingness? The other answer I hear to that is that the boundaries of the universe fold back on themselves in the manner of a circle to form a sort of sphere. Fine. Is it floating in something? Is sitting on something? If it is, then what is that? If it is not, then I really have a problem.

I believe that the answers to these questions are above the line. They are in the domain of God. Two thousand years ago when the Romans ruled much of the western world, there were no airplanes, but the concept of flight was clearly in their grasp. Today I doubt we are much closer to defining infinity than Caesar might have been. We have a good symbol for it in the horizontal figure eight, but whether you draw it on a page or inscribe it in the air it still has boundaries.

It has been said as an argument for the existence of God that it is impossible to view a fine watch without understanding that there must certainly have been a watchmaker. I believe it is equally impossible to imagine any watch able to understand the nature and complexities of that watchmaker.

The point is that had God never chosen to reveal himself to us, we would know absolutely nothing about him. I realize that in earliest history man created a number of gods, but I am speaking of the God who created man. It seems impossible then that the nature or person of God can be found at the end of a mental exercise no matter how logical, no matter how well directed and powerful. What we can have is a measure of God's grace in such quantities as we are willing to sit quietly and receive it. Understanding? That is something reserved for when we each escape the restraints of time, space, and the limits of our intellect.

Chapter 22: *Last Leg*

It's 0530, and though the sun is still below the horizon, I can see daylight looming. In the young hours of the day most sailors are anxious for dawn. This day was far from being an exception.

We were off the Florida coast on the western edge of the Gulf Stream with a modest southwest wind that together with the current pushed the boat over the bottom at around 6.5 knots and through the water at 4–4.5 knots. We were still some 108 miles from the St. Simons sea buoy, and at this speed I would have to enter the harbor at night. I had done it several times before with no problems; I could certainly do it again. However, I had motored up the waterway all the day before. Then we negotiated the bridges and the lock exiting the Canaveral Inlet at dusk accompanied by a line of squalls. We continued on through the night and had a full day left before St. Simons. I could always duck in at Fernandina before dark, but I was going home. And home I would be tonight. I'd have a cold one at the dockside bar.

Raise the Sails

If I fired up the Yanmar, speeds over the bottom in the 9 plus knot range would be easy. Trouble was the diesel tank read empty on my remote gauge and the gauge mounted on top of the tank occasionally bounced off the E as the fuel sloshed around inside. A flashlight assisted visual inspection was inconclusive. I felt certain that there were several gallons in there, but how much of that would be accessible I had no idea. I wasn't about to burn the last of my fuel in the middle of the Atlantic. This was a sailboat, after all.

So the plan was, if daylight ever arrived, I would set the cruising chute and a current assisted 9 knots over the bottom was almost assured. However, there was not a chance that Captain Oakley would allow an attempt at a spinnaker set in the dark. He had appeared last night and insisted on a double-reefed main with the thunderstorms lurking in the area.

"Safety second, sailor!" He had been adamant. "Captain Morgan first." Captain Oakley can sometimes be bad to drink.

"What's that, sailor?" Captain Oakley emerged from the companionway. "I got to put up with insults from some greenhorn not fit to be called a seaman? About out of fuel? I'm not surprised. What kind of seaman heads out of port with near empty tanks?"

"A broke one, sir?" I rubbed my eyes, Captain Oakley had looked strange earlier in the night, but now I thought I detected a seediness to his appearance that he had failed to achieve before.

"Broke one, my backside, boy! Oughta have you flogged." He tried to contain a rum redux belch. "Lucky thing for you I got business to attend below!"

When light did arrive, I rolled up the headsails and raised the chute, still safely stowed in its sock. The sheets were run down either side of the boat and I had the main let out hoping to blanket the chute a bit until I had it fully released. I pulled on the sock halyard that lifted the collar to the head of my sail. The collar slipped up nicely, and the spinnaker began to fill from the bottom upward until it happened. The collar got stuck either halfway up or half down. The point of view here is irrelevant since either way is completely unsatisfactory. OK, I'll douse it. You guessed it. Now the blasted thing refuses to come down. With much effort and some strong language, I manage to get the sail down and stretch it out somewhat in the lee of the doghouse. I wrapped the lower portion of the sail with a spare line to keep it from filling and sweeping me and whatever else might be in its path overboard. Now that everything is within reach I am able to raise the collar by hand with zero problems. More wraps of line to secure the upper portion of the sail and it's ready for try number two.

Up she goes again. A few tugs on the jury-rigged control line and she set with a rumpling whoop of nylon. A little trimming and our boat speed began to build. Soon the knotmeter says 7.7 and the GPS reads 10.1. At this rate I'll be there for happy hour.

We're cooking. I go below and check the batteries: they still read about 12.8 volts, so I should be able to run the autopilot and anything else I want with amps to spare. The problem now, aside from breakfast, is an optimum course from a speed of transit point of view.

Raise the Sails

The Gulf Stream never gets much closer than 70 miles off the Georgia coast. It would not be prudent to run a straight line to the STS Buoy, nor wise to follow the Gulf Stream until due east of my destination then turn to course. After some study I determined that when I was 85 miles from a point in the center of St. Simons Sound I would steer for the channel.

This left me three hours to confront the problem of breakfast. I solved that problem by thawing out the last beef filet from stores I'd picked up in Stuart. I had hoped for a dolphin, but at this speed I was not likely to get a strike.

An hour later with a stomach stretched tight by beef and potatoes, my mind fell to what I might do next. Sailing had opened new doors to me, and I had acquired skills and experiences that guaranteed that my life would never be the same again. When a little thought is applied to the state of things prior to becoming Sid the Sailorman, "never the same again" began to sound like a mantra of hope. What would never the same again include? Some things that it should not include came readily to mind. But what would I do. I knew I would need a job. Sailing had not paid well, and it was past time to make a deposit into the old bank account.

"Include?" A voice overripe with sarcasm erupted from below. "What will my life include?" Captain Oakley burst up the companionway and threw his gritty commodore's cap on the cockpit deck. "You make me sick! Wallowing around up here stewing over your future like some sorta dang fool!"

Captain Oakley looked different this time. Instead of his normal British Navy uniform he was dressed like a scruffy yacht club reject who had possibly earned a living fishing for cod, but had caught more whiskey than fish. A couple of prominent skin cancers and a heavy stubble of beard completed the picture. I remember being thankful that I couldn't smell his breath. Maybe the change in his appearance could be explained by this being the first time I had seen him in full daylight. He couldn't be my Ghost of Sailing Future. Could he?

"What's your life gonna include?" Evidently he was not going to leave me alone. "You're thinking it'll include some of them magical postcard sort of moments, or that somebody will actually want to read some of that drivel you've been writing. Well, I'll tell you what life's got in store for you, boy. It involves a deep fat fryer and a paper hat if you don't get off your butt and stop feeling sorry for yourself. So get used to it!"

Captain Oakley spun around stomped down the companionway steps. Halfway down he stopped and came back. He snatched his hat from the deck.

"That's my damn hat!"

He disappeared down the companionway, and thus far I haven't seen him again. It is a sad thing to admit that you have to conjure up hallucinations to tell yourself the truth. I have tried therapy and can report that it is only somewhat more gratifying, only marginally more effective, but substantially more expensive.

I finished my last leg under spinnaker. Sometimes I would steer, but mostly I let the autopilot have the helm. I avoided the whiskey bottle, opting instead for a bottle of rust remover. I spent much of the day polishing the stainless steel to a like new gleam. *Silk Purse* would need a lot of spit, polish, and varnish to get her in shape.

As I finished shining up the last stanchion, I noticed tears dripping from my jaw line. A moment later, I was sitting with head in hands and tears flowing freely. At first, I wasn't certain of the cause, and then slowly I realized that for the last several hours I had been cleaning *Silk Purse* as the first step toward putting her on the market. She would bring a fine price. I might even make money against her purchase price, but it felt like selling a best friend or a child. She had been ever faithful, but soon she would no longer be a necessity. *Silk Purse* had done her part toward my redemption. She had brought me to a place where I could finally listen to the voice that had been speaking to me most of my life. Now she was a luxury that I could no longer afford.

One night back in Milledgeville, Georgia, I sat in the choir loft and tuned God out of my life in favor of whatever pop culture station had been in vogue. I had finally come to realize that it wasn't life that I had been running from, or even life's responsibilities. I didn't want to admit what was missing in my life because to do so would mean that it wasn't Judi's fault. It hadn't been my father's fault. I couldn't blame it on the legacy, or the fact that I had lost a portion of my childhood. It was me.

So now you know that *Silk Purse* really didn't save my life; she simply carried me to a place where I could sit quietly and listen. Sit quietly and receive a measure of God's grace. It is an activity that I highly recommend.

Late that afternoon I saw a tiny post floating in the water just about where the St. Simons Sea Buoy should be. A little bit further and my thoughts were confirmed. Our course had to be adjusted less than ten degrees west for *Silk Purse* to sail up the center of the ship channel. It was low tide and tourists played on the beach in front of the King and Prince Hotel. A little farther and we were in the mouth of St. Simons Sound. I doused the spinnaker a hundred feet in front of the village pier with more tourists pointing. This time the sock worked to perfection. Ten minutes later the chute was stowed away, and we sailed to within sight of the Golden Isles Marina before I dropped the main and motored into my old slip.

Chick was there to catch my lines, just as he had been many times before. Nothing here seemed changed, but inside me a seed was growing.

Lesson: "Now you tend that seed, sailor!"

Chapter 23: *Update*

Judi and I are back together. All our problems did not vanish, and a few new ones have replaced some of the ones that did go away. This time, however, they are our problems, and we have begun to realize that problems can be transitory if we face them.

Old Scratch will still occasionally crawl on my chest and offer the promise of the legacy.

"Come on. Come on."

Now when I feel him whispering in my ear, I try to focus on the new seed in my life that has sprouted and grown to a small bush that hopefully will one day be a tree.

Silk Purse is sold, and I miss her. With the passage of time, I have come to accept that she was a possession, not a member of the family. She did prove to be well named though. Back when I was waiting for her to arrive, I decided to use Doug's suggestion of *Silk Purse*. This name came in a small way from the early Island Packets being referred to by some as island piglets. This was a way of thumbing my nose just a bit at that moniker, but I like to think the name *Silk Purse* also had echoes of our mother's voice.

"Life can be a silk purse or a sow's ear, just depends on the choices you make."

It has been several years since the night I was visited on the Bahama Banks. I remain more convinced than ever that the conclusion I drew then was the right one. God has become active in my life, and as a result my value system has undergone a radical shift. Concepts I once thought silly and merited only scorn are now held close to heart because that night on the Bahama Banks my entire frame of reference changed.

I have not heard another clear voice in my head. However, on those occasions when my mouth is shut, and my ego has its head tucked under its wing, I am favored with a small measure of God's grace.

I can now look forward to having another sailboat someday, only this time she won't have to save my life. By now you realize that I believe God reentered my life on a perfect night of sailing. What I am just now realizing is that he was there all the time; I just had to shut up and listen for him.

Today I wonder if, in my rebellion, I have missed the life that was planned for me. Possibly, I will never know that. But I do know that I can't fix the past; I can only move forward. Life is a one-way street and there are still many forks ahead. This time, with God's help, I hope I make the right choices.

Maybe I'll make some more silk purse decisions.

Sid Oakley

Disturb us, Lord, when we are too well pleased with ourselves, when our dreams have come true because we dreamed too little, when we arrived safely because we sailed too closely to the shore. Disturb us, Lord, when with the abundance of the things we possess we have lost our thirst for the water of life.

Stir us, Lord, to dare more boldly, to venture on wilder seas where storms will show your mastery, where in losing sight of land we shall find the stars. We ask you to push back the horizons of our hope, and push us to the future in strength, courage, hope, and love. AMEN.

Sir Francis Drake

GLOSSARY
Sailing as a Second Language: *It's easier than French*

Abaft   Toward the rear or stern of a vessel. An older term similar to aft.

Abeam   At a right angle to a vessel.

Aft   Toward the rear or stern of a vessel

Astern   Behind the vessel.

Athwartships   Across the ship

Back 1) To trim a sail to weather, windward. 2) A counter-clockwise shift in the wind direction.

Beam   A vessel's greatest width.

Bilge The lowest part of a ship's hull, generally equipped with pumps for removing collected water.

Block A nautical pulley.

Boatswain, bo's'n or **bosun** The crewman in charge of rigging, sails, spars, and anchors.

Bowsprit A large spar extending forward from the bow or stem of a vessel used primarily to attach headsails.

Bobstay A stout support, generally made of chain or a solid metal rod, running from the bowsprit to the leading edge of the hull to counteract the force exerted on the bowsprit by head stay tension.

Brace A line used to control the horizontal settings of a yard (cross spar) on a square-rigged sail.

Brig A two-masted vessel with a fully square-rigged foremast, the lower mainmast supported a fore-and-aft rigged sail.

Brigantine A two-masted vessel having a square-rigged fore mast and a fore-and-aft rigged mainmast with square sails on the upper mainmast. Often called a jackass brig.

Bulkhead A vertical and often structural partition in a vessel.

Close-hauled To sail as close to the direction of the wind as is efficient. Beat, beating

Coaming The deck like portion of a boat just above the cockpit seat.

Cruising Chute A large light weight asymmetrical sail used for light air sailing especially down wind

Dead Reckoning (D.R.) The determination of a boat's position based on course and distance run.

Draft The distance between the waterline and the lowest point of the keel. The depth of water required for flotation.

Fast Secure. As to make fast a dock line.

Fathom A measure of six feet used to determine depth.

Fore-and-aft rig Having sails rigged lengthwise to the vessel as opposed to across the boat as in square rigged. Performs much better to weather, toward the wind direction.

Fix A vessel's position based on at least two bearings.

Forward Toward the bow or stem.

Furl To roll up and secure a sail.

Ground Tackle Anchor, anchor chain and/ or rode and attendant gear.

Gunwale A vessel's rail or upper planking at the edge of the deck. Pronounced "gun'l".

Halyard A line used to raise a sail and keep it up.

Harden up To head up, steer toward the wind direction.

Hard over As far in one direction as possible.

Header A wind shift requiring the helmsman to steer to leeward (away from the wind) or the crew to trim the sails.

Heading Course.

Head off To alter course leeward, away from the wind.

Head up To steer or alter course windward, toward the wind direction. Also "come up," "harden up."

Hull speed The theoretical maximum speed of a displacement vessel obtained by multiplying the square root of the waterline by 1.34.

Jibe To change to another tack by moving the vessel's stern through the wind. Also an older term, wear.

Kedge-off To use an anchor to pull a grounded boat into deeper water.

Knot One nautical mile per hour.

Larboard Older term for the left side (facing forward) of a vessel, port side.

Lee The side or direction away from the wind.

Lee Shore A shore down wind of a boat. Can represent a clear danger when anchoring orsailing too close

Leeward   Downwind. Pronounced "loo ward" or "loo ard."

Mainsail   The sail hoisted on the aft side of the mainmast. Pronounced mains'l. Also, main.

Nautical Mile   Approximately one minute of longitude. 6076 feet or 1.15 statute mile.

Piloting Navigating a vessel when in sight of land.

Pooped Struck by a wave breaking over the stern. One reason for the high structure and deck on the stern end of old sailing vessels.

Port The left side(facing forward) of a vessel. Larboard.

Porthole   A small window. Port.

Preventer   A safety line rigged to prevent the boom from swinging across the boat in case of an accidental jibe

Quarter Deck   A deck aft and above the main deck from which an older sailing vessel was commanded and steered. Aft deck. The popular name for watering holes along the east coast.

Reef To reduce the size of a sail to accommodate stronger winds. Often the main is reefed as night falls night as a precation.

Raise the Sails

Rode   The line connecting an anchor to the boat often nylon three stran roped, but can be chain or chain rope combination

Schooner   A two-masted vessel fore-and-aft rigged.

Sheet   1) A primary sail control line. 2) To trim a sail.

Shrouds   A set of stays made from rope, wire ropes, or rods leading from the upper mast to the hull that support the mast.

Sloop   Single-masted vessel, generally with one headsail and a main sail.

Spar   A stout pole used as a mast, mast section, yard, or bowsprit.

Square-rigged   The principle sails are rigged across the centerline of the vessel and held aloft and extended by yards fastened to the mast. This arrangement makes the vessel efficient off the wind.

Starboard   The right side (facing forward) of a vessel.

Stay Sail or Stays'l   A smaller jib cut sail set on an inner forestay to allow a variety sail combinations. Very popular with cruising sailors.

Tack To change the direction of a vessel by turning her bow through the wind until the wind blows from her other side.

Sid Oakley

Yard A long spar hung from the masts to extend square-rigged sails.

Yardarm Either end of a yard that extends past the mast.

"Just try to be as seaworthy as your boat, if you want to be a sailorman."

Captain Oakley

Acknowledgments

This book is dedicated to Judi. I wish I had nine lives to spend with you.

It would be criminal not to acknowledge my brother, Doug without whom this book would have never been conceived or written. Doug was my sailing mentor and best friend through the most difficult and yet rewarding time in my life.

I wish to thank the people of the Exuma Bahama Islands and everyone at Island Packet Yachts for their inspiration and help with this effort.

Finally I would like to thank my editor, Riina Hirsch who has made this a much better book than it otherwise might have been.

About the Author

Sid Oakley spent his early years in the shadow of the steeple of a small Methodist church in a lower-middle-class-redneck neighborhood in southwest Atlanta. Like most around him, he grew up with one hand on the Bible and the other entwined in the chains of racism. His mistake in later life was to believe in order to reject racism he must surrender his religious heritage. His experiences in the Exuma Islands taught him otherwise.

Today he describes himself as a refugee from Augusta, Georgia, and lives and works in the Atlanta area with his wife Judi and their child Gable the wonder Chow. Sid continues to write, dream of the sea, and enjoy his new life and friends in St. Martin's Episcopal parish.